SETLIFE

Setlife Publishing
www.setlifebook.com

Printed in Australia

First Printing, 2016

ISBN 978-0-995-3584-0-9

Edited by:
Jenny Webb
www.themicrowavejenny.com

Cover Design & Internal Illustrations:
Allan Wrath
www.bamboostudio.co.nz

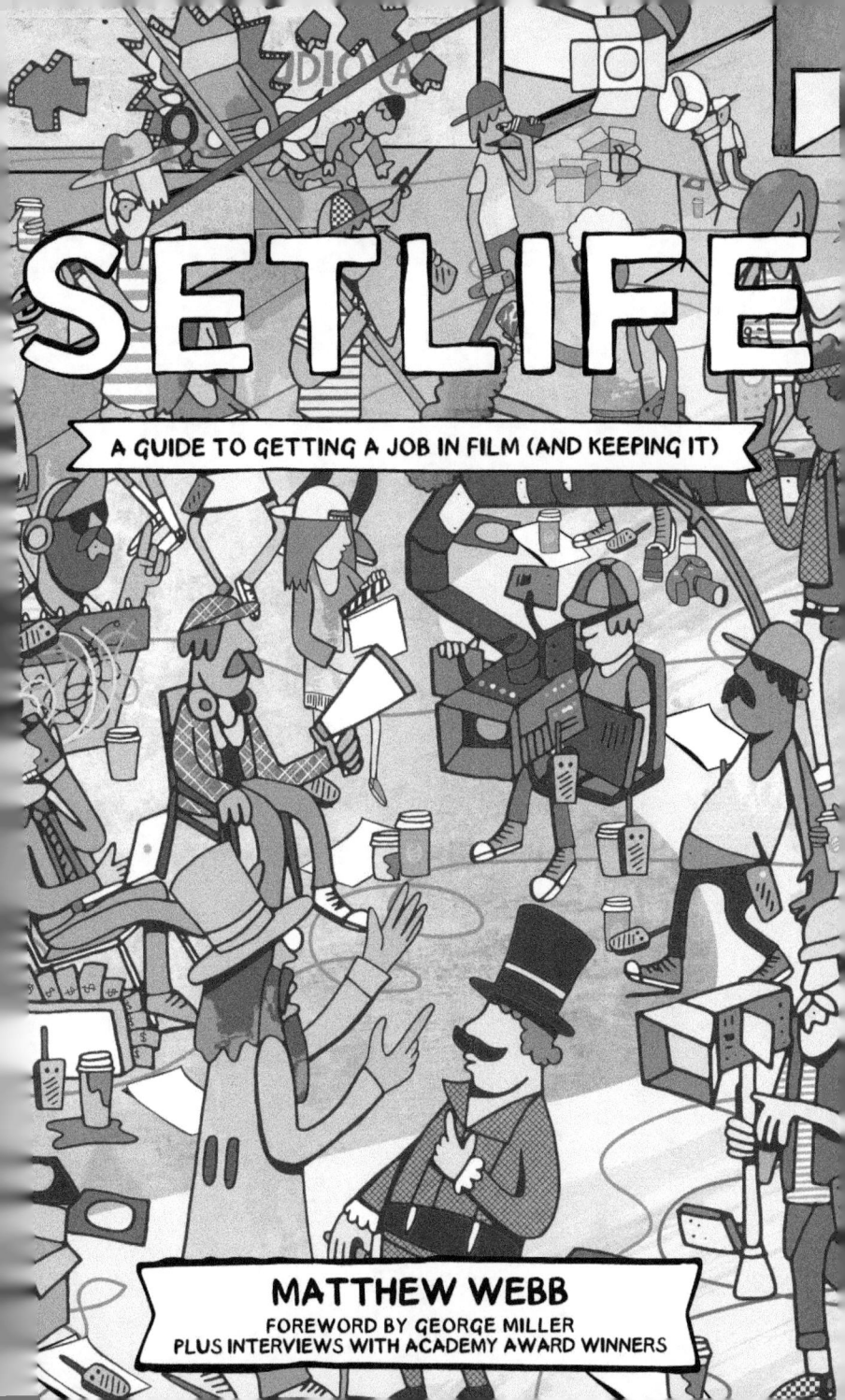

SETLIFE

A GUIDE TO GETTING A JOB IN FILM (AND KEEPING IT)

MATTHEW WEBB

FOREWORD BY GEORGE MILLER
PLUS INTERVIEWS WITH ACADEMY AWARD WINNERS

CONTENTS

FOREWORD
BY GEORGE MILLER

Film sets are an extremely strange environment to walk into, let alone continue to thrive and evolve. Matt has been a keen and observant contributor to many elite crews and major productions. His book, *Setlife* is a valuable guide for anyone looking to build a career in the film industry. Film schools are wonderful in teaching you film history and the practicalities of filmmaking but this book delves deeper into what working on a film set actually involves and how to excel in this field.

ABOUT
GEORGE MILLER

George Miller directed, wrote and produced *Mad Max: Fury Road*, which brought his iconic post-apocalyptic title character back to the big screen. In 2016 it was nominated for 10 Academy Awards and received 6 wins. He won an Oscar for *Happy Feet*, and was Oscar-nominated for *Babe* and *Lorenzo's Oil*.

INTRODUCTION

1

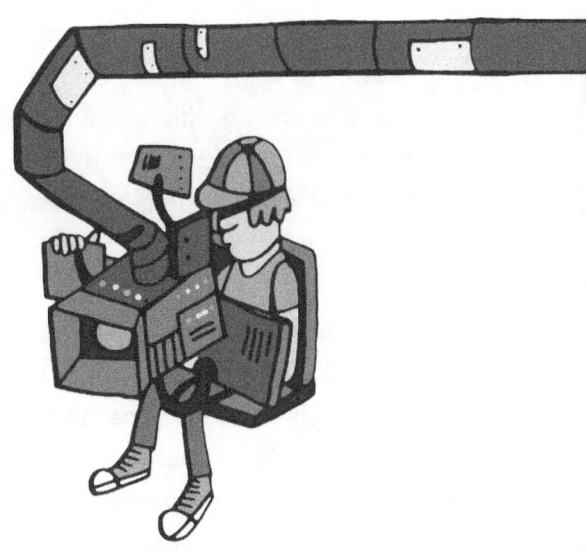

So, you've finally finished film school. Or, you've accrued years towards other pursuits and have suddenly realised your future involves movies. Now comes the daunting task of getting a job in what appears to be the hardest industry in the world to crack. The saying, 'it's all about who you know, not what you know' definitely rings true, but this book will help you both nudge that foot in the door, and keep it there in an industry that requires the highest level of work ethic.

Based on my personal experience, this book explains exactly what to do on set, as well as the things you should definitely avoid. It's a compendium of everything I wish I had been told before I took my first job and stepped onto a fast-paced, working film set. From the outside, a film set can be intimidating with lots of people rushing about, seemingly knowing exactly what is going on and using a smorgasbord of strange terms. *Setlife* will prepare you to not only nab that first job, but build a stellar career.

Where do I stand? How do I ask for help? How can I help when I don't know what is going on? How do I use this radio they just threw at me? These are the questions that you will struggle with in your first experience of a film set. This guide is designed to reveal all that happens in a day at work and how best to approach becoming an integral part of a functioning set. It will help you if you are studying, have just landed your first work experience, or even if you have a few projects under your belt already. I don't claim to be an expert in the field, just somebody who has gone from studying at university to work experience to landing my first job and now establishing a career as an Assistant Director.

I've worked with a lot of interesting people, some difficult people, wonderful creatives, and have shot in many challenging locations. I've been involved with small films and the biggest films. I still have a long way to go and continue to learn more every day. I have been fortunate to learn under some great teachers and mentors who have taken the time to teach me exactly what is expected of my role. Unfortunately, this doesn't always happen as this takes time, and the most precious commodities of a film are time and money.

Film schools and universities are a great place to develop your skills but they can't teach every little nuance that happens on set and how to juggle life and a career in film. One of the biggest struggles working on a film is that it demands so much of your time that it can put a strain on your social life and relationships. The following chapters will give you an insight into how to deal with this pressure in order to achieve a work-life balance.

Throughout the book I've included interviews with multiple Academy Award-winning filmmakers and crew. Their insight into the industry over several decades provides priceless advice and direction for developing filmmakers. All their experiences have been different, showing there's no 'one way' to develop your career, but that hard work is always rewarded if you keep pursuing your passion. Each individual shares specific information relevant to their department but all have a common understanding of filmmaking and the teamwork that is involved in producing a film. I hope you enjoy reading their personal experiences as I am thankful for how open and honest they have been with me.

I suggest you flick to the back and have a read through the glossary before starting the next chapter. The film industry has many specialised and unique words and phrases, so understanding them before you step on set will be extremely helpful. I use them throughout the chapters so it'll help you along the way if you know what all these terms mean.

Good luck with your own career and endeavours. Things won't always turn out the way you expect, and sometimes you won't get the job you think you deserve, but the alternatives can be just as good, if not more exciting. It's a competitive industry but everyone looks out for each other and before long, you will have a newfound film family.

Welcome
TO THE FILM INDUSTRY

2

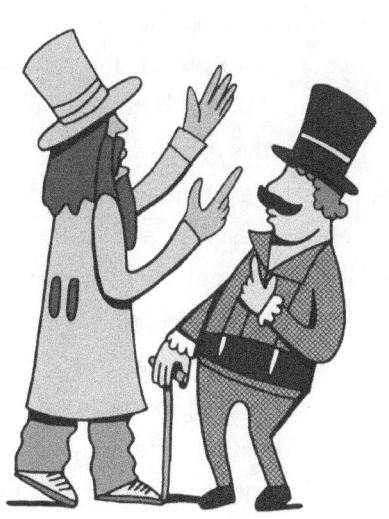

GETTING WORK EXPERIENCE

The proverbial 'foot in the door' idiom is often elusive and can seem intangible for a burgeoning film mogul like yourself. The rumours are true: it *is* actually all about who you know. Rejection may be rife as you circulate CVs and monotonously cold call in a bid to jam just a pinky toe through the doorway. But once you discover your pre-school best friend's auntie's boss' dog trainer is the daughter of an Assistant Director on Hollywood blockbusters, things suddenly shift. That is the phone call that matters.

The truth is, the majority of work experience and jobs will come from either people you already know or friends of friends of people you know. There's no harm in cold calling and emailing your CV to production companies, agencies, crew members and studios, but the response rate will be much lower through this method. I'd still recommend doing this because maybe the timing will be perfect when your CV lands on someone's desk. It's also good practice for when you will be doing this to get the next contract.

Pursuing work experience while studying is a savvy idea and can lead to promising longer term prospects. Some colleges and universities offer practical subjects that necessitate attachment to a film or TV show. Immersing yourself in the environment of a larger working film set will help you gain contacts, give clarity on which direction you'd like to head within the industry, and set you up with that additional insight that could result in the perfect role. Work experience while studying is much more attractive to productions, as you are usually covered by your university's insurances and thus aren't a burden to the production. You will need to check this with your appropriate university or school, but it is common practice.

Internships are a no-brainer to gain hands-on experience, and are a great path if you are able to sustain yourself financially in other ways. Some internships are even paid at a low rate to relieve some of the financial burden. It's always best to have some goals of what you want to learn and achieve from the internship, and if this is not being satisfied after a few months, don't be afraid to move on to something more suitable. When you're a spring chicken you generally don't know what you want, even if you think you do, so enjoy observing all aspects of the film process as a litmus test to determine what suits you best. Internships can be juggled while still studying, and many are available to graduates during their numerous breaks.

But of course, back to the obvious problem at hand – you don't know anybody in the industry! You feel like Christopher Nolan could be your number one dinner party guest and you'd get along perfectly, but you don't always operate in reality. I didn't know anyone when I started my degree – in fact, I wasn't even the typical cinephile waxing lyrical about my favourite Italian directors and thoughts on the Dogme 95 movement. I just liked making movies and wanted to learn how to do it better. It took time and effort for me to meet the right people and to develop these relationships.

Once your pinky toe wedges its way into a little open nook, no matter how small, how unpaid, how seemingly insufficient – be appreciative. Even though you write like David O'Russell yet inconceivably get placed in the Costume Department laying out fabric, or you know you can manage a set like it's no one's business but you find yourself carrying shot bags for the grips, it's okay. You'll still see how a film is made and gain a valuable understanding of the processes involved in creating two hours of screen time. Everybody's path to his or her dream role is different. Some people fluke it and ride the coattails of success for some inconceivable, unidentifiable reason while others inject blood, sweat and tears into carving out a name for themselves. Typically, you'll find the latter is more realistic. And that's okay, too.

To illustrate the idea of carving your niche in action, my work experience was organised while I was studying at university, initially attaching me to the location department of a TV drama. The role was advertised in our film course newsletter and I applied immediately. I had missed a similar role the previous semester as I was too late and it had already been filled before my email went out. It was an unpaid, full-time role for two weeks and I was covered by the university's insurances so all I cost the production was the food I ate on set. I arrived day one expecting to 'scout locations' but was reassigned to the set, where I was escorted by the friendly Location Manager who believed I would get more out of the experience this way. He introduced me to the Assistant Directors (ADs), wished me luck, and opened a door for me to experience something exciting, fun, and coincidentally right up my alley. I've worked as an AD ever since.

During those two weeks I was polite, asked questions, was always early to work, enthusiastic, tried to show initiative, and when I was taught one job I continued to do it each day, like getting water for the cast and Director. I owe a lot to the three ADs that really took me in for those two weeks and showed me what it's like to work in the industry. It wasn't exactly what I imagined before I started, and wasn't even what had been organised and discussed with my teachers, but it turned out to be the right place for me to learn.

Here are some simple tips to help you get that elusive work experience role or internship, succeed at it while you are there and hopefully turn it into paid work:

1 EMAIL AND CALL EVERYONE.
Anyone you know that has a connection to the film industry. I was speaking with a girl I worked with in my retail job who's father was a Sound Recordist. He passed on some details of people I could contact. Nothing ever came of it but that was the only

connection I knew of in my circle of friends and family to begin with.

2 EMAIL AND CALL SOME MORE.

Contact any production company with a decent slate of work. TV work experience is easier to come by as more content is produced in a shorter timeframe. This means that free help is generally appreciated. Clearly state details such as timeframe, possible departments and if it's part of a subject you are studying.

3 SPEAK WITH YOUR TEACHERS.

They may have relationships with production companies they send interns to each year and may be able to recommend you to these companies.

4 SEARCH THE WEB.

Search all the major production companies and studios websites for job advertisements. There are hundreds of opportunities out there but they fill up fast so make sure you apply as soon as possible.

5 GO THE EXTRA MILE.

Just because you aren't getting paid doesn't mean you can sit around and be slack. Ask questions so you show a keenness to learn, show initiative, be early every day, stay until the end of the day, and get to know them; you don't need to talk about yourself too much.

INTERNSHIPS DON'T PAY THE BILLS: TURNING WORK EXPERIENCE INTO A REAL JOB

Work experience and internships are great for translating theoretical knowledge taught at film school into everyday practice. Preliminary detective work, however, reveals the obvious – it often doesn't help pay the bills. The novelty of two-minute noodles and boxed dinners has an expiry date, and so does your ability to continually work for free.

You might be one of the lucky ones – landing a job as a result of your work experience or internship. For most, however, this is likely not the case. Most jobs in the industry aren't advertised traditionally; I've actually never received a film job in a conventional way by submitting a CV or application. Frankly, it's all about reputation. When a Head of Department (HOD) is looking to crew a project, certain names will be thrown around in discussion for positions. The difference between getting offered that role or not rests in the immediate response of trusted individuals when your name is raised. If positive, you will more than likely get a phone call and a meeting. If negative in the slightest, you won't be contacted unless they become desperate and are struggling to fill the position. Construct your reputation through developing great character – through the way you conduct yourself on set, your language, your work ethic, your presentation and how you relate with the rest of the crew.

I was lucky enough to be offered a full time position soon after my work experience ended on the TV show. The 3rd Assistant Director (3rd AD) was leaving mid-season to go onto a different job so a position was available in the New Year. Was I ready to fill those shoes? Definitely not. I had two weeks of real film production experience under my belt. For some unknown reason (maybe they could pay me less than everyone else), the Unit Production Manager (UPM) offered me the 3rd AD role. There were more experienced candidates available but I had the advantage of two weeks of insight into that show. I already knew the cast and crew, which would be a slight advantage later on.

I spent another month shadowing the ADs on set every day, learning and absorbing their skills and tasks. I aimed to benefit them so they would give me tips and help train me in return. I took a small amount of pressure off them by doing simple tasks such as making coffees or looking after extras when needed, and they would hang around for fifteen minutes at the end of the day and explain certain responsibilities of the job to me. My two weeks of work experience that was supposed to be with the location department became six weeks of training and then a full time job as a 3rd AD on a TV drama. Many friends have also shared similar stories with me about their first foray into the film industry. All are unique and everyone has a different experience of getting that coveted job.

The usual process for being offered a role is a phone call from someone in a superior position or a UPM explaining the project, estimated dates and pay. Typically, people employ crew they have either previously worked with or who have been recommended. It's important to be working in the right circles for each type of project (but more about that later).

Earlier I said it doesn't matter what role you get placed in for work experience or your first job. However, once you are in, you need to start pursuing positions that will lead you where you want to end up, otherwise you might find yourself inexplicably doing hair styling even though you're bald and have never done a braid let alone brushed your own locks. If you want to be a feature film editor, there's not much point being a driver for a reality show. You won't get offered assistant editing positions from this. Be deliberate and purposeful in the roles that you chase to build your pathway.

NEGOTIATING A DEAL

Negotiation is a learned skill for most. It is nerve wracking and awkward, but necessary in the industry. For every job you will have some kind of negotiation over pay rate and conditions. Negotiation for a job takes place with the UPM or HOD, and definitely gets easier in time. Asking for more money or dealing with a UPM you don't know can add to the stress, but you will eventually learn to navigate these conversations with finesse. Initially, you won't have a lot of bargaining power, so a tip is to more or less take what is on offer. However, time and experience will sharpen your resolve to bargain for what you're worth, not what you're offered. Nevertheless, be mindful that being employed for less than you had hoped for is usually better than no employment at all.

Here's some simple tips to get you through your negotiations:

1 Know what your position gets paid. If you go in knowing what you should be offered for that position, you will know how to react when they state an amount. This can be hard when you first start out because it's not really kosher to ask people what they earn for their position. Many of the unions publish market rates so I'd suggest doing some research on their websites to see what each position is expected to be offered.

2 If it's your first time in this role you are more than likely going to be offered a low rate. We've all been there. So as long as it's a good opportunity and you are working with a great crew, don't worry – it'll get better as you gain more experience.

3 Make sure you are in the right frame of mind to negotiate. I often get called while I am on set but discussing my next contract while juggling three-hundred extras is not the right time. I ask them if I can call back at a later time when I can be in a calm environment.

4 Politely comment if the rate is below what you were expecting and make it clear what your expectation was. You can always suggest what the union's market rate is, so you were expecting something closer to that ballpark. You may need to inflate your rate marginally in case you have to negotiate down slightly from what you have stated. If you are on par with the industry rates they will generally come to the party (if the budget allows).

5 Remember that the UPM has to negotiate with most of the crew and occasionally the cast, which can number in the hundreds. For them, the shorter the better. Keep your discussions short and state your requests clearly. Don't play games and hopefully they won't either.

6 Don't worry if they start telling you there's not enough in the budget, everybody's taken a pay cut etc. It's the same story on every job. Know your worth but don't be greedy. You will discover your rate will differ slightly depending on the scale of the project. This is normal, and allows small and independent projects to be made.

7 Getting the job is probably more important than arguing over $50 a week if the UPM is someone who may give you more work in the future.

8 You don't have to agree immediately. Once the discussion has settled, I often say I'll have a think and let them know my decision the following day. This allows me to discuss the job with my wife and decide the pros and cons of doing the project.

9 You won't get every single detail in that initial phone call or meeting. Realistically, you'll probably only discuss a weekly deal based on a fifty-hour week (this comprises of forty normal hours and ten hours at time-and-a-half pay), a rough start date and the length of the job. This is also the time to discuss any box rentals such as laptops or tool kits, and vehicle rentals.

10 Once the negotiations have been finalised, you can ask for a brief email confirming the rate, box rentals and dates so you have it in writing if the negotiations took place over the phone.

After you've negotiated a rate and details, you will be issued a deal memo. This normally happens during the first week of work, or occasionally you may receive it before you start. Your deal memo will generally be based on a standard industry contract (otherwise you should have discussed it in your initial negotiation with the conditions of work stated). The deal memo is the basis for a crew contract that is undertaken between yourself and the production company for the period of the project or timeline discussed. Very exciting and professional-sounding, no? The drudgery of the process is redeemed by the realisation: you've landed yourself a job on the path to achieving your dream!

I've had straightforward negotiations, hard negotiations and negotiations that have broken down and resulted in me not doing the job. From each experience I have learnt something and have improved at this process each time. These days when I'm negotiating, I can go in confidently knowing what I'm worth and can back it up with previous job rates. Some people are better at negotiating than others, but you will not be able to avoid this part of work life so you might as well get used to it and become good at it.

DAY ONE

You may have stayed up until 1am trying on every possible outfit you own to make a great first impression. The sad truth, however, is that although the film industry is sold as a glamorous one, the red carpet is the only place you'll find any of us looking adequately suave.

On set, things are as practical as you can get. I remember the very first day on work experience trying to figure out what jobs all the people did based on what they were wearing and how they acted. I could spot the DOP, the 1st Assistant Director, the Producer -- but I couldn't figure out who the Director was. I was hoping he was someone spectacular. Is Spielberg in today or is Scorsese directing this episode? The Director usually resides behind the monitor but the homeless man standing there didn't fit the bill. He had on an oversized black t-shirt (either an on-trend Ksubi shirt with fashion holes all over, or literally just a twenty-year-old rag). I think it was the latter, and complementing the look was an elastic waistband that once connected to the rest of the underwear, hanging out from his pants. His bum crack was on display for all the crew between the overused undies. 'That is the Director?!', I thought with incredulity and awe. I was neatly dressed in chinos, a button up shirt and dress boots and he looked like he hadn't showered in weeks.

That's the amusing thing about film sets. It's all about practicality (admittedly personality played a part too in this instance). Meanwhile, for the rest of us crew who want to maintain some form of dignity while still keeping it simple and comfortable, here are a few basic guidelines:

1 COVER YOUR TOES

This is a big concern on set. I'd hazard a guess that I could rock up entirely naked bar a pair of sensible, covered shoes and the safety officer wouldn't bat an eyelid as long as I'd passed safety regulations. Whatever your role on set, make sure you wear covered footwear or you may be asked to leave. Serious stuff.

2 COMFORT YOUR TOES
Make sure those covered shoes are the comfiest pair of shoes you've ever walked in. After standing up for twelve hours straight, you'll hope your feet are walking on clouds. When working outside, I generally wear hiking boots because they are supportive, waterproof, grippy and last a long time. I won't win fashion points, but I still come up trumps on the Director who sometimes doesn't even have laces in his shoes. When on the sound stage, I wear good runners as the concrete floors will wreck your joints, so a good cushioned shoe is best. In my role as an onset AD, I average between 15-20 kilometres of walking per day. In fact, we track this seriously – it's a competition! The highest I have seen by an onset PA was 38 kilometres. Doing that in dodgy shoes will destroy you.

3 SLEEVE UP
I personally wear long sleeve button up shirts because I like the sun cover they offer. Either cotton or linen is breathable and keeps me as cool as a cucumber. I never wear white because it ends up a strange shade of brown by the end of the day and it's never ideal meeting with the Producer on wrap in a sweaty, brown stained white shirt looking like a slob.

But maybe I'm just grubby and white would be fine for you on set.

4 KEEP IT PRACTICAL

Stick to comfortable shorts or pants. It goes without saying that skirts reveal problems (and undies) once up a ladder. Even though you might think your role doesn't involve anything physical, the one unfortunate day you do wear something inappropriate will be the day you inadvertently surprise the entire crew with more than you bargained for. It's a bit boring and limiting, but practical clothing is the only way on set.

5 SLIP SLOP SLAP

A cap or wide brimmed hat is crucial when it's sunny, as is sunscreen. Protect yourself from UV rays and sunstroke. You'll be grateful to skip both.

6 PACK A RUCKSACK

I always keep an overnight bag in my car with spare items such as an extra rain jacket, t-shirt, shorts, undies, socks, shoes and a towel. This is for the random days when we get asked to stay on location or for when your clothes get muddy, wet, torn or someone else needs to borrow a spare item (hopefully not your undies though).

When you repeatedly rack up long hours in the conditions we work, you won't care that you sort of resemble a parking ranger. You will look for comfortable and practical clothing, and you'll wear it with pride and confidence. This practical dress code will enable you to do all the demanding and physical activities your role requires – and you won't regret it.

Now to your actual first day. A classic day one will begin with you arriving at unit base with a five-pager containing the nuts and bolts of what's happening, and you not understanding half of it. Welcome to the call sheet. Luckily there was a map and you're pretty sure you parked in the right area. You may be introduced to your new department or you may already know a couple of the crew. It feels like you are starting high school all over again but the class went back weeks ago and you are a late entrant. It's breakfast time and you have a few hours to prove to the other crew members you aren't a waste of space slowing them down in the lunch line. I mean this. The first day is critical. You walk a fine line of being over confident or way too shy, not having a clue what is going on but trying to stay involved, and you have forty new names to remember when they all buzz around at a million miles an hour. Worse, you keep finding yourself in the way of people moving equipment. It's okay. We all started there not knowing what to do.

The first day will feel long, as realistically you won't have anything to do. Continue to ask your department how you can help throughout the day without being an annoyance. Offer to get them a tea or coffee at appropriate times. Note: You need to be a master in this realm -- learn your coffee and tea names, and practice getting good at making them. It will go a long way. Luckily I worked at a coffee shop as a teenager, but if you need to do a simple barista course to get up to speed, I'd recommend it.

Watch and imitate what the people in your department are doing and see if you can get involved helping. It may take a few days for them to check you out and trust you, and also discover that you can be of help to them. At appropriate times, ask questions about what they are doing or what something means. Sometimes you may not get an answer if people are too busy but generally people will get back to you and give you time when they can. Everybody learned from watching and asking questions at some stage in their career so most people are open to passing on the information and training the next generation when the time is right.

Aim to remember people's names and what their role is in the first week. Odds are they'll forget yours but don't worry about that. If you can address them by name when asking them a question they'll appreciate it. To help with this, you can get a crew list from the production office or from the ADs. In my first few jobs I would go through this list when I had a minute on set or at home testing myself on who I knew and who I didn't. I'd keep this in my pocket so I could do a refresher on set when needed.

Once you get through day one, the rest of the week will be slightly easier. You will get to know the crew better each day and will be surprised how well you get to know them in a short period of time. In this first week, make the effort to be early and stay until the end. If your call time is 0700, get there at 0630. It shows you are keen and ready to help, whatever it takes. I can't emphasise how much coming in early still helps me with my role. You may find someone in your department explains a lot of things as you help them set up, or they may invite you for a beer after wrap with some of the crew. It's these crucial moments that can be missed if you only do the minimum of what's required.

SOME STEREOTYPES TO AVOID

Often the biggest problem stopping new or inexperienced crew continuing to get work is their attitude. Sometimes it is the fact that they just can't fulfil the job, but most of the time it all boils down to their attitude and how they approach the tasks. There are many negative stereotypes that emerge on set during work experience or from junior employees, and I can guarantee if you start to display these characteristics early on you will struggle to find employment. Here's what to avoid when starting out.

THE KNOW-IT-ALL
Congratulations on winning the prize for best cinematography at your university's film festival. However, don't parade this fact around in front of everyone on set

with your superior knowledge and opinion because, well, no one really cares and you are possibly now in a new league of experts. Nobody begs to work alongside a know-it-all. There's nothing worse than a new person on set who cannot be taught and doesn't listen to instruction because they think they already know everything. They have the arrogance of thinking they should start at the top, and are not prepared to put in the hard yards of starting at the bottom rolling cables or making coffees to learn from the more experienced and skilled professionals.

These know-it-alls don't last long on set. Often they are ridiculed behind their backs and hung out to dry when it is inevitably revealed that they, just like everyone else, do not actually know everything. How do you avoid being 'that guy'? If a crew member explains something to you, let them finish their sentence before you cut in with your own thoughts. They may say something you didn't expect, or teach you something you didn't already know. Even if you find you do have the upper edge on some of your peers, adopt the rule of 'know-it-alls finish last' and be courteous anyway. It will dramatically improve your road to respect.

THE SHY ONE

A film set can be a daunting place at the start. You might try to talk to some people on set but the 3rd AD shushes you because the cast are blocking the scene. Each department runs with their own jokes, and everybody seems to have friends at lunch. So where do you sit, and who will listen to your top-notch banter? It is easy to become removed and shy and let the opportunities pass, but this will not lead to jobs in the future. There is a delicate balance between being ostentatious and overbearing, and timid and reserved. Get to know your department and learn to observe the best times to chat to them. The rest of the time, focus on the work at hand and your actions will be noticed and appreciated as you prove you are a hard worker.

Make sure you are memorable but not for the wrong reasons, and aim to be personable and outgoing rather than whisper quiet. Before and after work are the best times to get to know your fellow department members as they will be relaxed and open to chatting without the pressures of the shooting schedule. Be bold at lunchtime and sit with some people you don't already know. Introduce yourself and start a conversation.

GENERATION Y

This generation gets a bad rap on film sets, but as a member of the group myself, we do sometimes fit the stereotype perfectly. I've seen twenty-somethings start their work experience or first job on set with electric enthusiasm as they finally get to do what they've always dreamt of. Soon, they realise that fetching coffee and rolling cables wasn't exactly what they figured a twenty thousand dollar post-grad cinematography course would afford them. They become dejected, unwilling to do these small tasks, and usually sit down behind the Director's monitor, just enough in the way to annoy everybody.

Out comes the phone and its zillion social media platforms as the bored Gen-Y does what they can to sustain themselves for the next four minutes because the Director inexplicably wants to do another take of the shot! Like three hours hasn't been long enough! Truthfully, film sets can be polar opposites within minutes. One minute they are crazy-busy with the whole crew involved in setting up a shot, and then for the next hour nothing happens while the scene rolls for up to twenty takes. It takes effort to keep concentrating when nothing's happening, but as soon as you get distracted is when you'll be asked to help out and you won't know what is going on as your head is buried in your latest status update.

My advice:

1 Don't sit down on set – it looks lazy and portrays you as someone who is willing to let others pick up the slack. This is especially important when doing work experience or on your first job. Just don't sit down – make it a rule.

2 Don't pull your phone out constantly and check your social media – it looks bad and appears as though you are disinterested and bored. If this is an issue, turn it off or leave it in your bag.

3 Enjoy doing the simple tasks. Making good coffees or happily carrying the heavy cases to and fro will be noticed and appreciated by your superiors even if you don't think they've seen you.

THE BIG EGO

There's no place for egos on set. This person is similar to 'the-know-it-all' but generally just thinks they are awesome without any validation of formal training or achievement. The film industry may hold the promise of fame and glamour, but you'll soon find out that the shine and glow is limited to red carpet premieres and award ceremonies. There's not much glamour in stomping around in foot-deep mud when it's been raining for the last three weeks or carrying equipment up sand dunes in blistering heat while you shoot desert scenes.

Nobody wants to be dealing with your ego on set, especially when you are first starting out (when you've won an Oscar you might be forgiven). You're there to do a job, that's it. If someone asks you to do something but you don't want to, get over your ego and get the job done. Some of the most recognised and awarded people I've met have been the most humble and accommodating. As a result, the crew strives for excellence for this individual, as they are well respected and genuinely nice.

Mark Huffam
Producer

The Martian, Prometheus, Alien: Covenant,
Saving Private Ryan

What was your first job in the film industry?
I was a runner for an election program on the BBC for 3 days. I literally had to run up and down the stairs between floors 3 and 7 when the elevator didn't work with messages.

Did you study?
No. I started working when I was 17 or 18.

What is one piece of advice you would give to someone starting in the film industry?
Make good tea and coffee. And never be late.

Did you think you'd be doing what you do?
Absolutely not.

What has been your favourite job?
Saving Private Ryan. I was relatively young when I got the job as the Production Manager. It was a steep learning curve but the time of my life. The production ran off adrenaline and this amazing energy. We shot the film in 59 days.

What's one piece of advice for potential producers?

Pick the right team. If you do the right preparation, the filming becomes easy. Choose good material to work with.

How do you approach working with high profile directors and cast?

Sir Ridley Scott is the best-prepared Director around. He makes it easy for me. The whole process becomes streamlined making everything easier.

What
DO I DO ON SET?

3

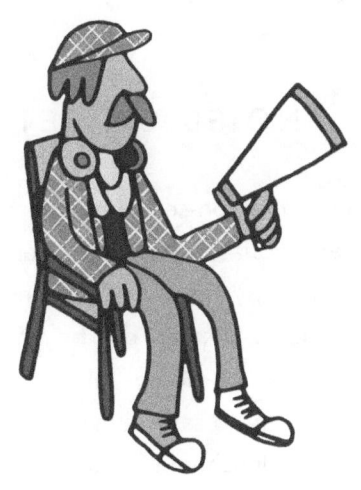

There is an unspoken law on set to which all crew either consciously or unconsciously abide. Every department is responsible for certain elements of the process and each crew member completes a series of specific tasks every day.

Film sets are based on a hierarchy of positions where safety and efficiency are top priorities. Those at the top aren't there to flaunt their power, but rather are more experienced and therefore justified to instruct their departments on how to achieve the vision of the Director. Every set will have a different balance depending on the scale of the project and temperament of the HODs. This hierarchy is not concerning, but you just need to be aware of this structure and how you fit into the overarching scheme. Over time you will learn this unspoken code and naturally function within appropriate boundaries.

NOISE ON SET

If there's one crucial on-set faux pas to eliminate, it's talking at inappropriate times. The embarrassment of being reprimanded by the 1st AD during a rehearsal, or more catastrophically, filming, can be difficult to redeem. If you are so inclined to do so, talk out of range and be sensible about it. I try to save my weekly catch ups or *The Bachelor* recaps to lunchtime, as that is where I can chat freely without the concern of missing something said over the radio or annoying those working quietly around me. As you get more comfortable on set, you will be able to navigate this appropriately and find plenty of time to chat with friends. Until then be aware of when and where you are talking on set. As a general rule, keep quiet when next to the cameras, cast and the Director's monitors. This is where the bulk of decisions and discussions are had and nobody appreciates the loud mouth distracting everyone from the task at hand.

If talking on set is a dire move, consider the grating intrusion of a ringing phone during a take. Keep yours on silent or off at all times. If and when this accidentally happens, proceed to your nearest liquor store for a case of beer as an act of repentance and peace offering to the crew. You'll be sure to hear someone calling out 'Slab!' when this occurs.

HOW TO USE A WALKIE TALKIE

You will be given a radio and will be expected to know how to use it to communicate with your department. Nobody likes wearing a radio. It's difficult to listen to one person talk to you, while you hear other people talking over the radio stuck in your ear. It will take time to adjust to this but a radio can save time and is an effective way for people to communicate across the set.

Each department generally has its own channel except for the ADs, Art, Costume, Makeup and Safety, who often all use channel 1 together. If using channel 1, it is important to restrict only necessary conversation to that channel. Anything that is specific to one person or lengthy in explanation is best served by channel 2 or another designated chat channel. This reduces the amount of unnecessary dialogue that is constantly in people's ears and keeps the channel free for any immediate contact. On set, I find myself talking to people through my radio more than face-to-face. It's important this communication is clear and precise so instructions don't get warped or lost in the process. Inevitably they do and this can result in some amusing situations, but can also result in someone else being extremely frustrated with you. Don't mumble, don't use superfluous language and just get to the point.

Radios aren't just for talking but also for listening to instructions and keeping up with what is happening. Depending on your department, most of the information to go about your work will be said over the radio via a superior or another department. Train yourself to listen when you hear these voices so you don't find yourself asking dumb questions that have already been answered seconds earlier.

Some tips on how to use your radio:

1 Speaking - Push the button and wait half a second before talking. This ensures that the beginning of what you are saying is not lost, as it can sometimes take a moment for the radio to start transmitting.

2 State your name plus state their name, et voila! Simple, transparent communication is achieved. E.g. 'Matt to Sam'. Wait for their response... E.g. 'go ahead' or 'hello'.

3 You now have their attention and can ask what you need. If you don't initially get their attention they could be speaking to someone face to face and won't catch anything you say. It's not rocket science but it is crucial to efficiency on set.

4 If your conversation is going to take longer than a couple of sentences, then best get them to switch to channel 2. This is done in the same way by getting their attention. After they have responded, you simply say 'switch to channel two'. They will usually respond with 'switching'. You can now speak freely on channel 2 but don't forget to switch back to channel 1 when you're finished or you will miss all the important info rolling around.

5 Note – channel 2 isn't a private channel. Many people will eavesdrop on these conversations if they think it involves them or they are just bored of the regular channel 1 talk. Don't go stating all your innermost secrets.

6 Speak slowly and clearly, holding the microphone about twenty centimetres from your mouth. You don't need to yell into it but make sure you are projecting your voice rather than mumbling.

7 It is best to keep your sentences short and simple so you aren't wasting time on the channel. This involves thinking about what you need to say before engaging in a conversation over the radio. You may find yourself saying some funny things when everyone is listening if you don't think before you speak.

8 When it's windy outdoors be particularly careful to shield your microphone when you are speaking so people don't think you're scrunching cellophane over it and pretending the line doesn't work. The small microphone is very sensitive to wind and nobody will understand you through the whooshing sounds.

9 Eventually your battery will die. Fresh batteries can be found in tubs scattered around set or if you're desperate and in a hurry, the ADs usually carry spares on them.

10 Take care of your radio. Charge it each night in the truck and try not to get it wet when it's raining. There's nothing worse than a faulty radio that is preventing you from communicating and listening to your department when the set is moving at a million miles an hour.

When starting out, it's extremely important that you understand how to use a radio effectively. If you are unable to master a simple task like this, your department will banish you immediately and deem you a useless cause. It's harsh but true. Alternatively, if you nail this within your first week and can be relied on to listen and communicate effectively, you will become an invaluable part of their team.

NO JOB TOO SMALL

One of the things I find most interesting on a film set is the attitude that there is no job too small. By this I mean it doesn't matter what position people are in, they are still happy to do the little things that help the project get made. The crew is made up of this strange balance of hierarchical departments and titles, but at the end of day, everyone is there to make the same project and work as a team. This attitude to the 'little stuff' is a triumph on most film sets, and so you want to be somebody who starts out with the same attitude, and maintains it even when you're the top dog.

Although the media may portray the film industry as largely ego-driven, the majority of crew including the world's best directors, DOPs and producers are typically humble, genuine people who have moved through the ranks over a long career. I've seen a 1st AD on a $200 million film jump in and shovel mud with the art department just to help save time and get the job done. I've witnessed producers help carry the ridiculously heavy dolly up flights of stairs with the grips because they are there to help. I've seen DOPs carry gear up and down steep mountains, as it's a team effort to get in and out of there as soon as possible.

On the flip side, I've also seen PAs roll their eyes when they are asked to do extremely menial tasks like get another department a coffee or clean up the kitchen. It all gets noticed and even though sometimes you may not want to empty the bins as it's not really your job, just do it. Make sure you maintain the attitude of lending a helping hand to other departments, as some days you all just help out whoever is struggling the most and one day that someone could be you. Thinking, 'it's not my job so I'll just leave it' is not what will advance you in your career. It's easy to stand back and let everyone else pick up the slack, but if you show your bosses that even though it's not your job to do that trivial task but you do it anyway, they will appreciate your work ethic and continue to invest in you.

DON'T TAKE IT PERSONALLY

You will get yelled at. It's a fact. Yelling is purely a reality of a fast paced workplace where time is money and the long hours result in the erosion of filters and enhancement of opinion. You need to learn to not take this personally. Like, seriously – it's not personal. Generally, the person who is momentarily loose-lipped doesn't even realise what they have said but are focused on what they are trying to do.

It could be the DOP or Gaffer telling you to clear the light when the 1st AD has just asked you to move some set dressing. It may be the 1st AD telling you to hurry up when you are waiting for the Director to finish telling you what they want done. It may be your department head just blowing off some steam and unfortunately you are in the wrong place at the wrong time. It's hard to brush it off as you may have been busting your gut all day for no recognition and yet still get criticised for something you had nothing to do with. It can be unfair, but unfortunately it occurs quite regularly. Stay focused on why you are there and know that you are doing a good job.

When the shoe is on the other foot years down the track and you are the tired HOD, be careful not to snap at the rest of the crew. I guarantee there will be times when you are tempted to. If you do happen to blow off steam at someone, don't be afraid to apologise, and quickly. The simple gesture of an apology goes a long way, particularly to junior employees. I have always appreciated apologies and been conscious of handing them out myself when things don't go how they should have. On the odd occasion when someone's issue is valid but the delivery is off, try to see past their yelling and take on board the criticism to make you better at what you do. Don't make that mistake again, and hopefully the person will handle the situation better if similar circumstances happen again.

And one more time for effect – don't take it to heart when someone mouths off at you. Hold your head up, think positively and continue doing the great job you're there to do.

WORKING WITH OTHER DEPARTMENTS

Although you are working for the same production company on the same project, it can feel like departments are working only for themselves and don't care about the broader picture. They can become disconnected from the wider project, as each team reports to their own HOD. There will always be people dedicated to merely executing the bare minimum required of them, and so you won't always receive the support or common courtesy when you most need it. Therefore, it is paramount to build a strong rapport from day one with everyone you encounter from other departments so that you can fulfil your role to your highest capacity.

Learning people's names and taking an interest in their role will get you leaps and bounds ahead when you need help lifting gear or ask for a small favour to get the task done. It goes without saying that you will reciprocate by always being available to help others if you want to build strong working relationships. There are enough uncooperative grumps on set – don't let yourself be typecast as yet another. Of course, film sets demand long, tough days and so rather than constantly being a Judging Judy, give people the benefit of the doubt.

Respect that good relationships are crucial to, and directly correlate to, your performance in your role and the overarching success of the set. For example, you will need to use or move someone's gear at some point, but don't expect that people will be impressed about it if you haven't handled the situation correctly and proven yourself to be decent and friendly. Once you do build stronger working relationships with people and are comfortable moving trolleys, you can typically do it yourself. Still, let them know you moved their equipment as a courtesy so they know where to find it. This is also particularly important for set dressing and props. If in doubt, just ask before you move it. Sure, the above sounds like a simpleton's guide to basic common courtesy, and yet… just don't be a jerk.

WORKING WITH THE DIRECTOR

Depending on your department, you will most likely need to speak to the Director on occasion. It is best to double check with the ADs on set and let them know what you need to do, as they will gauge the right time and sometimes quickly extract some time with the Director themselves if it is important. There are some extremely inappropriate times to approach the Director with questions and if you find yourself interrupting at the wrong time – beware! You may find yourself berated in front of the crew.

Pick your moment by observing the types of conversations they are having at the time, ask what you need to ask efficiently and make sure you get an answer as often they'll get pulled in a different direction before they give you what you need. Just before or after lunch are generally good times to ask questions for future shoot days. Sometimes you need to know about props for the next scene or how you should be setting the background extras, so it's important you build rapport from the start of the project to get your answers in a timely manner.

In pre-production, get to know the Director so they are aware of who you are and what you do. They are relying on you and your department to make their film, so they should be approachable and interested if what you are saying is directly related to the film. Each and every Director will be different and you will form different relationships based on this. Some will be heavily interested in the job you do whereas some may leave it up to you to make decisions. You will get a feel for this during pre-production and can tailor your approach to suit.

WORKING WITH THE CAST

Talking with the cast can be daunting at times but becomes part of everyone's job as you progress into higher roles. As with talking to the Director, it is all about timing. The cast can be extremely easy to work with, or they could be the very definition of impossible.

All departments will at some stage have to ask an actor to do something, whether it's a Focus Puller requiring the actor's mark, an AD getting them to travel to set, or Standby Props giving them the props for the scene. Use common manners when addressing them as it'll always go a long way even if they aren't that pleasant in return. Make sure you have their attention before rambling on about the scene or nonsense. It's awkward to have them look up and say, 'Oh, sorry were you talking to me?'.

Get to know their name even if they don't know yours. Sometimes you will build a strong rapport with the cast, particularly if you have worked with them on other jobs, or if you are on a TV show that has done multiple seasons. However, for the most part, I find actors are fairly reserved on set. They may keep to themselves, generally because they are constantly practicing their lines, or they could be a method actor and thus keeping in character and trying to avoid anything that may pull them out of their world. Over time you will make some great friends with the cast and you will also discover people you will happily never see again in all your days. Every project has different egos and cast hierarchy. Play the game and get your job done well. Don't be smarmy, but be professional and effective.

STAY OUT OF ACTOR'S EYELINES

An eyeline refers to where an actor is looking in the scene. It may be directly at the other actors, it could be out to the horizon or it could be an imaginary moving car that is driving in the distance.

The Director, DOP and Script Supervisor will discuss shots to make sure the eyelines are consistent and match when they shoot the coverage. The actor may be given a separate mark, which can either be a real actor or simply a marker on a stand. This eyeline may be different to where they were looking in previous setups in the scene depending on where the cameras are now positioned and what looks best for that shot. The consistency of an eyeline when cutting between shots in post is crucial to avoid looking like the subject the actor is focusing on is constantly moving. You will hear the eyeline described in relation to the camera. E.g. The eyeline is left to right. This means they should be looking from camera left to camera right. It's often amusing to hear the Director and DOP argue about eyelines and where each actor should be looking. It can be a confusing subject and often they are arguing the same side.

So, why should you care? To stay out of it, is why. Actors are performers and they need to feel secure during filming, so you cannot step through their eyeline. You'd likely not love fifty people gawking while you feign 'true love' and awkwardly kiss your sweaty co-star in a claustrophobic studio. Such a kiss could only be made worse by a wandering PA aimlessly ambling into their line of sight. Actors often find themselves out of their comfort zones in front of a film crew consisting of hundreds of people. This demands huge amounts of energy not to be distracted by something happening in their periphery. Sometimes large black curtains will be setup for privacy or the set may become a closed set in the case of nudity or sex scenes.

If you need to be close to the action during the scene, try and hide yourself behind some equipment or set dressing so that you remain inconspicuous. Alternatively, turn your back to them or simply look down at the ground while the scene is played out. Don't move around and fidget.

For the majority of crew, all you need to know is to stay clear of the eyeline while filming. If you are an aspiring DOP, make sure you spend time studying and understanding eyelines and how it works in the edit room as one day they'll be looking to you for the answers and you might even get your chance to prove the Director wrong.

WORKING IN TIGHT SPACES

In film land, you are inevitably going to be squashed into terribly small shooting spaces that are hot and stuffy. At times, there will be no space for lights, cameras and equipment, let alone the twenty crew that need to be in the room at the same time. Working in these small spaces will test everyone's patience. It is also a proven way to annoy the crew if you don't know how to deal with this situation. Here are some tips to avoid getting in the way of others whilst breathing down their necks:

1 THE BARE NECESSITIES

Only take necessary gear into the space. Try and find alternative rooms to store your camera trolleys, battery chargers, standby kits etc. If it's not crucial to have it with you, store it somewhere out of the way.

2 SPACE CADET

Only be in the space when needed. Stand beside the doorway (not in it) or somewhere close where you can hear what is happening but aren't in the way. You could even let your department know you are just outside the door if they need you as there's not enough space for you to be in there.

3 THE SPOTLIGHT

Avoid finding yourself standing in front of lights or cameras. A sure fire way to annoy everyone trying to frame up the shot is to be constantly standing in the wrong place.

4 DRESS CODE

If you need time in the room to set dress or do costume or makeup checks on the cast, let the 1st AD know and they will give you an appropriate time to do this when all the lighting has been set and some crew can exit the room to create space for you.

5 **DOOR STOP**
Don't find yourself standing in the doorway. It may be the best place to see what is happening in the room but it's the only entrance and exit for the crew. Soon enough someone will barge into you carrying heavy equipment if you find yourself loitering there.

TURNOVER, SPEED, MARK IT, SET, ACTION

Hopefully by now, you understand that it's not all sparkle and shine in film land. You know how to act on set so that you aren't sent home before lunch on your first day, but there are a lot of specific processes that continually happen on a film set that you need to become familiar with. There is a specific flow to these processes – from rolling cameras through to action and cut. Crews execute this sequence hundreds of times daily, and it requires multiple crew members working autonomously and efficiently. Here is a breakdown of the process:

1 After the Director has blocked out the scene with either the cast or stand-ins, discussed the coverage of the scene with the DOP, built the camera moves such as a dolly or steadicam, set the lights and dressed all the props in, the scene is ready to be shot.

2 The cast will be invited to set and everyone will be asked to settle down and clear the eyelines.

A rehearsal may take place if needed for cameras, cast or the Director.

3 Makeup and costume will then be invited to do their final checks to ensure all the cast and extras look perfect and match previous takes.

4 You will hear the 1st AD call 'turnover', which means roll the cameras and sound recording device. They may alternatively say 'roll camera' or 'roll sound'.

5 The Sound Recordist will call 'speed', which means they are now recording. The term comes from when they used to record the sound to film and it took a little while for the tape to get to the right speed of frames per second.

6 You may hear in the background some other ADs relaying 'rolling' and 'quiet on the floor' to ensure the whole crew knows we are about to shoot and that it's important to be quiet and stop moving.

7 The 2nd ACs will then call the slate, i.e. '47 bravo take two'. The 1st AC will call 'mark it'. The 2nd AC will clap the board and clear shot.

8 The Camera Operator will call 'set', which means everything has been done and cameras are in position for the 1st AD or Director to call 'action'. Most of the time the 1st AD will call 'action', but in some circumstances the Director may wish to. During specific scenes, the 1st AD may hand over control to the Stunt Coordinator or Special Effects Supervisor. This is because the elements involved are either stunt or SFX specific and they are the best person to call 'action'.

9 The scene will then play out and the Director will call 'cut' at the appropriate time. This will then happen again, and again, and again... until you can't recall a time that you weren't on set.

Although this process appears to be quite complex, experienced crews have this refined to a tee so they don't waste time when filming. At times the order may be adjusted slightly to suit each shoot. E.g. When a tail slate is required, but this process is the standard for most crews.

For the record, a tail slate is when the slate is marked at the end of a take, as opposed to before action is called as per the usual process. There are unending reasons why this is sometimes necessary – the camera operator needs a pre-frame for the action, it's dangerous for the 2nd AC to be in the area as SFX have rigged explosives, it's an emotional scene so it suits the actors to do it after the take – plus plenty more scenarios you'll discover.

Lesley Vanderwalt
Makeup/Hair Designer

2015 Academy Award Winner (Best Achievement in
Makeup and Hairstyling) – *Mad Max: Fury Road*

The Great Gatsby, Moulin Rouge, Gods of Egypt, Australia

What was your first job in the film industry?
I started as an apprentice hairdresser in 1972 and was asked
to interview for a Makeup Artist at the local television station
by one of my clients. I had no idea what that was.

Did you study?
I did my hairdressing apprenticeship, which they allowed
me to continue at the television station once I started work
there. But did not study film or makeup. I learnt on the job.
There wasn't so much money involved in productions 40
years ago in NZ. There weren't even Polaroid cameras, so
you had to draw all your continuity images.

**What is one piece of advice you would give to someone
starting in the film industry?**
It is a long hard road, don't expect it to happen overnight and
have some money put away so you can choose your projects.

Did you think you'd be doing what you do?
No, I wanted to be a fashion designer but always loved
making or creating things.

How has winning an Oscar changed your career?
It hasn't changed at all, but you do have a feeling of reaching
the pinnacle of your career and wondering if I should retire –

just joking! It has given me a platform to promote our work in the industry.

What would you be doing if you didn't work in the film industry?
Sleeping! No, I think I would have liked to have been an Architect or maybe a Chef.

What was your favourite job or best memory?
Far too many to mention in a paragraph – each job has its own energy or journey.

What's so great about the makeup department?
Being at work before anyone else and finishing after everyone else apart from maybe the riggers! It's a very creative environment with great like-minded people and you play a very big role in the look of the film. You need the patience of a saint and selective hearing in some cases, you must be able to multi-task and have good stamina, boundaries and a sense of humour.

How does someone start out in the makeup department?
Usually as work experience from the makeup schools.

How do you approach working with high profile directors or actors?
Be polite and listen, listen, listen. You need to see their vision through their words and references, and give the actor the space to become the character he or she is portraying.

Quick Guide

TO SHOT COMPOSITION

4

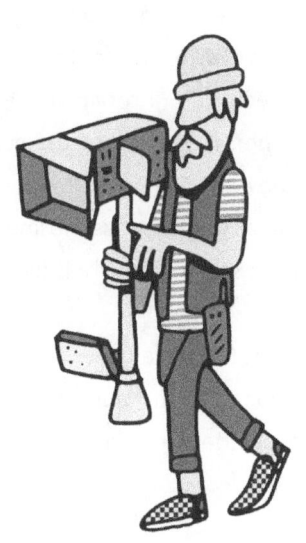

Even if you don't want to be a DOP or Director and aren't deciding the coverage of a scene, it's still important to have a basic understanding of how to compose shots and what rules need to be followed to ensure the scene can be cut together smoothly in the edit. You will find all departments using shot descriptions everyday explaining what is being setup so you will need a brief understanding of the terms. You may have studied this in-depth at college but here is a quick recap for those who may have slept in on lecture days.

THE 180-DEGREE RULE

The 180-degree rule, often referred to as 'the line' or 'crossing the line', refers to which side of the action the cameras are placed. For example, let's say you had a simple interview setup with an interviewer and subject sitting opposite each other. If you shoot the subject from the left side of the interviewer, the line is drawn along the left of the two characters. So as to 'not cross the line' you will then place the cameras on the same side when filming the interviewer.

If you were to shoot from the other side, having 'crossed the line', it would appear to the audience that the interviewer and subject are on the same side and is rather baffling to the viewer.

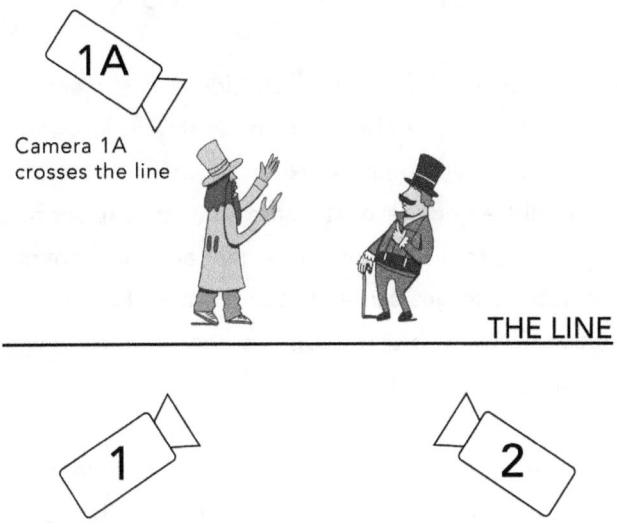

Camera 1A
crosses the line

THE LINE

This rule becomes more complex in scenes that involve lots of movement or multiple actors. The DOP will sometimes break this rule by starting on the correct side of the line and doing a camera move through the line to finish with the subject on the opposite side. This reduces confusion to the viewer as they see the perspective change as the camera moves. Most of the time you will not notice this while viewing unless it is dreadfully blundered, in which case you will likely laugh self-righteously.

A good little exercise is to watch a film and consider where the line can be drawn for each scene. You may even notice when the rule gets broken intentionally or accidentally. There's plenty of explanation online if you want to study this further, particularly for those burgeoning DOPs among you.

SCREEN DIRECTION

Screen direction refers to which side the subject enters or leaves frame. If a character leaves screen left and is in continuous motion, e.g. walking down the street, then they should enter the next frame from the opposite side (screen right) to ensure the movement appears continuous. If the subject leaves screen left and enters from the same direction (screen left), it appears they are returning to where they came from.

You can experiment with this by filming people entering and leaving from different screen directions. Then edit the footage to create different journeys with the same content. You'll notice directors using a mix of screen directions throughout films to create different perspectives of time. A mixture of screen directions in a montage will create the sense of passing of time and a large distance travelled.

SHOT SIZES

Shot sizes are regularly discussed on set so it's good to have a brief understanding of this so you don't look like a fool when you don't know what they are talking about. Shots can be described in multiple ways but often they will be defined by how much of the subject is in shot.

Here are the main terms that are used:

Wide Shot – the subject and all their surroundings are included in the frame.

Long Shot – the subject's full body is contained in the frame.

Mid Shot – the subject is framed from the waist up.

Close Up (CU) – a portion of the subject is in frame showing greater detail. E.g. A close up of the subject's face as they speak.

Extreme Close Up (ECU) – the frame shows only a small portion of the subject in great detail, focusing just on this one element. E.g. An extreme close up of an eye.

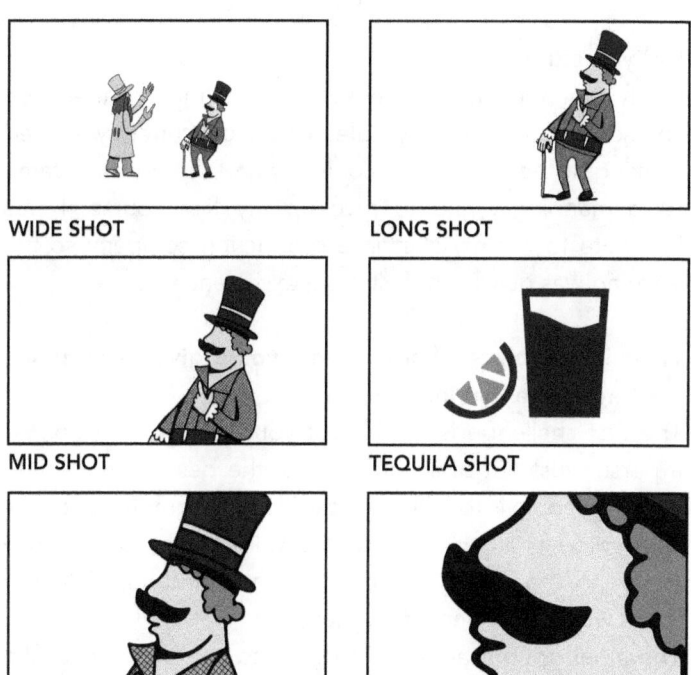

WIDE SHOT

LONG SHOT

MID SHOT

TEQUILA SHOT

CLOSE UP (CU)

EXTREME CLOSE UP (ECU)

Simon Duggan
Director of Photography

The Mummy: Tomb of the Dragon Emperor, The Great Gatsby, Knowing, 300: Rise of an Empire

What was your first job in the film industry?
I started as a trainee camera assistant straight out of high school. It was at Ross Wood Films, a production company that was fully crewed and equipped with stages, lighting, grip and camera equipment, and editorial facilities.

Did you study?
I only managed a few weeks with a Film and Television course at North Sydney Tafe. I had concurrently started working at the production company and the hours became so demanding I had to give up my film course. I was fortunate to get my start in a production company so the learning was quick with first hand experience.

What is one piece of advice you would give to someone starting in the film industry?
The first challenge is to just get your foot in the door. As a person just out of school, one of the best ways to meet camera people is to join the local Cinematographers Society as a student member. There you will have an opportunity to get to know many cinematographers and hopefully get some work experience from them.
The other options are to try to get into one of the local film schools. When you finally get the opportunity to get on set as a trainee it's important to make sure you engage the crew and be as helpful as you can. The crew will be watching you

and if they think you have what it takes, they'll consider you for further work.

Did you think you'd be doing what you do?
I had always been interested in photography through high school so I was motivated to find something related to the industry. I had no idea what the world of a cinematographer was so I had no clue where I would end up. One of my first interviews was at a tape duplication company – I was told I was not suited to the industry so fortunately I didn't get that job!

What was your favourite job or best memory?
One of my best memories was Director Alex Proyas inviting me to shoot the film *I, Robot* in Canada. It was my first US film and Alex had to work hard on getting the studio to accept me as the DOP. The shoot went very well and it paved the way for future US film productions.

What's so great about the camera department?
The fact that you get enormous satisfaction out of every learning step you take working up the rungs from Assistant to Focus Puller to Operator and finally to shooting your own work. Every day brings a new challenge and there is always a great camaraderie within the camera department.

Why would someone pursue a career as a DOP?
Firstly you need to determine that the film industry is for you, the hours are very long and you are away from home more often than not. Besides the obvious creative talent, you need good people skills as you are conducting an often-large crew of technicians. It takes dedication and determination.

Five Stages
OF FILM PRODUCTION

5
—

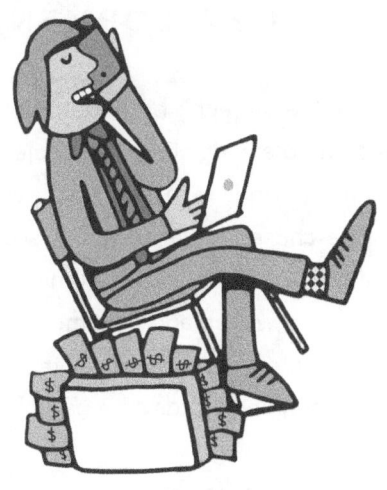

There are five main phases to the life of a project – development, pre-production, production, post-production and distribution. Each phase will have a different purpose, aimed solely at getting the project to the next phase, moving forward to distribution. You may only be employed for one of these phases depending on your role and projects will vary in length for each stage. Some projects may never even make it through all five stages with plenty of projects falling over in development and pre-production due to various circumstances. Although you will most likely only work on projects during a portion of pre-production, production and post-production, it's useful to have an understanding of all five stages and what is involved with each step.

DEVELOPMENT

This is where the project is birthed. It is the creation, writing, organising and planning stage of a project. In development, a preliminary budget is made, key cast are attached, key creatives are chosen, main locations scouted and multiple script drafts may be written. It's all the groundwork to show what the project will be and how much it will cost to make, and starts the moment a Producer thinks of a project or a Writer starts penning words on a page.

Development can take months or even years to get the project green-lit by a studio or funded independently and move into pre-production. Green-lighting a film means the studio has approved the concept of the project and will finance the project and move into production. Many producers have multiple projects in development at once in various stages of concepts. Some projects will get the green-light quicker than others and some may go through multiple script drafts and changes before the producers are ready to move into production. The crew involved in the development stage is quite minimal compared to all the other stages, as it's just a small group of creatives and executives crafting the story and associated budget. Once a project finds finance, it will move into the pre-production phase with an emphasis on shooting dates and time frame for the project to be finished.

Development can be extended or the project can be put on hold, affecting filming. The producers may be waiting for a specific actor or Director to become available, the climate to be right for shooting in the chosen location, or even new writers to make edits to the script. Alas, there are countless examples of films hitting roadblocks during development, resulting either in delays or folding entirely. A consequence of being employed by one when it is either delayed or goes under is that you quickly become jobless with little warning.

A particularly well-known example of troubled development was *Mad Max: Fury Road*. Development & pre-production on the fourth instalment of George Miller's Mad Max franchise, which first launched in 1979, began in the late 90s with a script penned and shooting planned for the early 2000s. A plague of bad luck followed. The Gulf War deterred filming in an initial scouted location, and when shooting was relocated to the barren landscape and perfect post-apocalyptic desert vibe in Broken Hill, Australia, a decade long drought broke. Dirt and dust were replaced with lush greenery and wildflowers. After over ten years of planning and delays, the film was finally shot in Namibia and South Africa, with pick-ups in Australia. During this time, George Miller directed both instalments of the Happy Feet films while waiting for the right time to finish his initial project. The film was released and received massive critical and box office success – proving that sometimes the wait can be worth it.

PRE-PRODUCTION

Pre-production (or 'pre' as it's called) is where scripts are amended, budgets are adjusted, actors are cast, locations scouted, crew employed, shooting schedule drafted, sets designed, costumes made and fitted, and everything to do with the shoot is planned and tested.

The pre-production stage can last many months from the initial green-lighting of a project to when cameras actually roll. As this date draws closer, the crew grows with many people being employed about two to five weeks before the shoot starts. There is a big push in these weeks to finalise everything that needs to be prepped before cameras roll. Although years of deliberation, concept moulding, writing and staring into space in a dreamlike daze is likely to occur in development, once shoot dates are confirmed the work becomes extremely focused on adhering to budgets and shooting schedules. The average pre-production length for TV dramas and films will range from about six to twenty weeks depending on the size of the project.

Subject to your role, you may get a few weeks of pre or just a few days to prepare for the upcoming shoot. This time is spent studying the script, testing and building gear, experimenting new techniques, fitting costumes, makeup testing with cast, and plenty of other activities aimed at preparing necessary items for a frantic shooting period. Although pre-production can feel a bit like the calm before the storm, if this time is used effectively, it will benefit the entire department so you won't be scrambling for last minute things as they pop up during the shoot (as much). You can't always be prepared for everything as things will change on every project but after a few jobs you will discover how best to use this time of preparation most effectively. Some people hate pre-production as they find it boring with too many meetings and discussions, but personally I enjoy getting involved in a new project and planning for the challenges ahead.

PRODUCTION

The production stage is where the rubber hits the road. The Writer, Director, Producer and countless other creative minds finally see their ideas captured on film, one day at a time. Production is usually the shortest of the five phases, even though it is paramount to the film and where most of the budget is allotted. The shooting length for feature films varies in length from about five weeks for a low-budget feature, and up to twenty-five weeks for a large blockbuster. TV dramas will vary depending on the number of episodes, but typically last from eight to sixteen weeks per season.

Production is the busiest time, with the crew swelling to hundreds and the days becoming longer in order to be as efficient as possible with all the gear and locations on hire. The crew works extremely hard during this period, with shooting hours each day ranging up to fourteen hours. Projects run to strict schedules with cast only contracted for a certain timeframe, so the crew is crucial in squeezing out every bit of energy to see the project successfully completed on time.

The production window is where most people in the film industry spend their employment. They are employed to get the film made and will go from project to project as each film begins production. The shoot period is the chance to put all your skills to the test and where you'll experience everything discussed in this book first hand. I find it the most exciting but also the most draining period of the process, although post-production can also be exhausting with long hours demanded to reach deadlines. Production involves amazing experiences, great people and the testing and development of your skills.

Actually calling 'roll cameras!' can be a real battle for filmmakers, and it is a big achievement to call on that first day. Although there is a long slog of shooting ahead for all crew involved, the film can pick up momentum as the crew starts to work well together and see the vision for the project start taking shape. It's exciting, exhausting and momentous, but the adrenalin combined with a stellar team can make the experience incredibly worthwhile, both personally and for your career.

POST-PRODUCTION

So you've thought of an idea, written a script, raised the funds, employed a bunch of crew to get it made, spent most of your budget and hopefully have shot some decent footage in the process. Now it's time to move into post-production. This is where the footage is edited, sound is mixed, visual effects are added, a soundtrack is composed, titles are created, and the project is completed and prepared for distribution.

Although the shooting crew has done a lot of hard work, now the post-production crew face arduous hours of work ahead of them to piece together the scenes and craft a stunning story. The Director, Producer and other key creatives have input while the post-production team work, but the responsibility lies with the Editor and sound mixing team to bring the film to life. Post-production will typically last about twelve to forty weeks, again depending on the size and style of the film. Animated projects or projects relying on visual effects will require more time in post-production as this is where more work is completed than in the shooting phase. Some animated features can take years to complete with hundreds of animators working on various sections of the film at the same time.

Rather than one big crew employed by the production as you see for the shoot, post-production is usually outsourced to a number of specialist film facilities that have the specific equipment to do the work. These facilities have editing programs, sound mixing studios, foley studios and colour grade suites with the latest technology worth thousands of dollars.

Post-production begins while the shoot is still going, as footage is gathered as soon as the first day of shooting commences. This helps see the project finished as soon as possible, but can also help identify problems with the footage or any gaps in the story while the shoot is still happening. If needed, shots can be picked up on later days without too much interference in the shooting schedule.

DISTRIBUTION

Without a stringent and robust distribution strategy, the other four stages of production are somewhat redundant, at least from a business perspective. Distribution is hardly considered by many working on the project, as they have no input or return from the results of distribution. However, distribution is the final stage in a project for producers looking to make a return-on-investment. This can be from cinema distribution, selling to a TV network or streaming service, or releasing direct to DVD. Whatever the distribution plan is, the producers will have spent many hours planning and marketing their piece to ensure the biggest audience and largest return. With the digital age and rapidly converging technologies, viewers are watching content in new and different ways, meaning that the distribution phase is constantly evolving.

Although distribution is the final stage of the project, the channel of distribution and marketing of the project will be planned in development and pre-production. If it is planned badly and fails to garner good distribution, then all the other phases will be wasted as nobody views the final product and covers the cost of the project. Hopefully, a project moves through all stages smoothly and efficiently and thus a Producer begins the cycle again on another project employing both myself (and possibly you!) once more.

Dan Oliver
Special Effects Supervisor

Mad Max: Fury Road, Pirates of the Caribbean: Dead Men Tell No Tales, Hacksaw Ridge, X-Men Origins: Wolverine

What was your first job in the film industry?
A film called *No Worries*. I was an SFX Labourer. The film had a few dust storms as part of the action, and I spent the film making sure all the V8 wind machines had a steady supply of dust to blow around. It was great fun. After that I became a SFX Runner/Buyer and then worked my way back onto set.

Did you study?
I studied Aeronautical Engineering for a couple of years – and although it's not directly related to the film industry it gave me a great understanding of physics and engineering, which is what SFX is all about. So it was not time wasted – I actually think my understanding of engineering gained at uni helped me climb the SFX ladder quicker than might have been. Once I decided to really pursue SFX I did an explosives course, rigging, and a few equipment licences. I've also received a Diploma of Film and Television with some of the diploma attributed to recognised prior learning.

What is one piece of advice you would give to someone starting in the film industry?
Sometimes it takes a while to get your foot in the door, so be prepared to start at the bottom. Make sure you can accept the lifestyle. It can be long hours and sometimes away from home.

Did you think you'd be doing what you do?

When I was at school I wanted to be a pilot. I hadn't thought about film and didn't even really know there was a job known as a Special Effects Technician. But as soon as I got my first look at SFX I liked it and wanted to pursue it.

What would you be doing if you didn't work in the film industry?

Absolutely no idea. Besides having a paper run while at Uni, and a small amount of builders labourer jobs, it's the only job I've ever had!

What was your favourite job or best memory?

Most memorable would have to be *Mad Max: Fury Road*. It was a huge practical effects job with a terrific crew. The film looked great and we (SFX crew) were all very proud of the work we did. And we were nominated for an Oscar and a BAFTA!

What's so great about the special effects department?

It includes many different disciplines – pyrotechnics/explosives work, hydraulics, heavy fabrication, model making softs and breakaways, and electronics. It keeps you interested and always learning.

Why would someone pursue a career in the special effects department?

If you like problem solving, building, fabricating and working in a team environment.

Features vs

TV vs TVCs vs REALITY

6
—

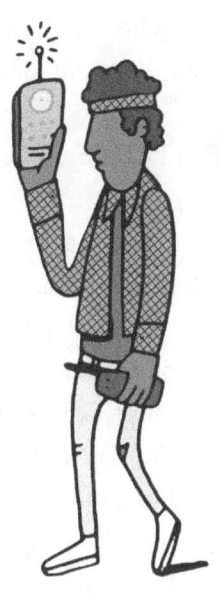

Like a lucky dip at a primary school birthday party, work projects and employment will sometimes take you on unexpected adventures. You'll enjoy getting to know different forms, lengths and locations. All these areas will utilise the skills you have in creating screen content whether for feature films, TV dramas, reality programs, game shows or TVCs. There are certain archetypal groups of people you'll find yourself working alongside depending on which stream of production you land. This does not limit you to working in this area for your entire career – it is possible to bounce between. However, I've found the more you do in one particular category of filmmaking, the more you will establish yourself in that arena and continue to be offered work there. Each stream has its own advantages and disadvantages but all are honing the skills you've developed and using them to create content for the screen.

FEATURE FILMS

Considered the cream of the crop for crews, feature films are where the best crews display their skills and can sometimes be rewarded with a highly acclaimed end result. Features can range from micro budgets in the hundreds of thousands of dollars, to massive multi-million dollar budgets, and everything in between. The differences between the small and large films can be immense, but at the end of the day, the principles are still the same.

Feature film schedules will range from about six weeks up to six months. There'll be only one to six minutes of screen time to shoot each day, so you are expected to always be at the top of your game and pour everything into those screen minutes. Thankfully, you will generally have more time to do a thorough job than you would in TV land so you can spend a bit more attention to all the detail in the shots.

Smaller films are an invaluable place to display skills you may have learnt from a stint in TV drama, as the schedule is more forgiving than fast turnaround TV. Large budget films can be extremely draining and involve very long hours, but the adventure can be a once in a lifetime experience. The work is often exciting, with large scenes involving hundreds of extras or thrilling stunts, which is why a lot of crew members love working on them. The pay rates are generally slightly higher on features than local TV production and the overtime can really add up as the weeks pass. Working on a large budget feature is an awesome challenge in whatever position you find yourself, and I'd recommend anyone who considers themselves a filmmaker to pursue a position on one of these projects and enjoy the wild tumult of little sleep and manic shooting days.

TV DRAMA

TV employs the most amount of crew, with networks pushing for fast and efficient screen content. New projects are constantly developed, renewed and revived, and many shows have multiple seasons. Often the shoots last three to six months and can sometimes run back-to-back with multiple series extending the schedule. The crew will shoot between six to ten minutes of screen time a day so the pressure is on to be resourceful and work in the most efficient ways. TV crews must operate like a well-oiled machine in capturing the show because there's not much padding in the schedule if they fall behind. The hours are long but can be slightly less demanding than feature films as the schedule is usually based on a ten hour shooting day.

Fast turnaround drama is a great training ground for young or inexperienced people looking to start their career or progress to a new position mid-way through their career. You will be regularly given new opportunities to prove your skills and will be tested every day on how to problem solve at a quick pace. Having said that, it can also be a brutal place to begin as everything moves at a hundred miles per hour and if you don't know what's going on or aren't confident in your role, you might be swallowed up by a jaded crew who feel they need to teach you a lesson. If you are up for the challenge, I'd definitely recommend having a crack at TV drama to establish your career and test your skills. I'm very grateful that I was trained in this environment, as I enjoyed the autonomy of learning on the fly and making mistakes along the way. I'm comfortable on a fast paced set and was taught how to time manage all the elements you find yourself juggling each day.

At the completion of the first season of filming, you may be asked to return for a second season or beyond, which can be highly enjoyable as you continue to work with a similar group of cast and crew. This can also be an avenue for people to move forward in their career as they move up positions throughout TV seasons. E.g. Someone who started as a 3rd Assistant Director may progress to a 2nd Assistant Director over the years of shooting a few series.

TVCs

Television Commercials (TVCs) are the highest paying per-day work, but the projects can be less regular and have very little job security. Some people choose to work mainly on TVCs as it allows them to work for three or so days a week and still bring in a good income rather than slogging out the long, demanding hours of feature films and TV dramas. This gives them time to see their families and have a better work-life balance. To continually work in commercials, you need to network and hustle with a variety of production companies and agencies to ensure you have projects coming in each week. This can take a few years to build up but once you have a large network, you can maintain a consistent level of work. Crews also love working on TVCs when they are between longer feature or TV contracts as it can give a nice boost of income without demanding too much time or energy.

A friend of mine once explained why he jumps between TVCs and features: 'TVCs are where the money's at, but you can't film fried chicken every day of your life and be proud of what you do'. TVCs allow him to bring in a solid income while still seeing his family, whereas feature films every now and again give him the opportunity to hone his skills and express his creativity within a longer form. Some TVCs can be great to work on with large scenes and interesting content, but for the most part, it is about making the ad as quickly as possible and keeping within the budget. This generally results in the crews being much smaller, with shoots lasting sometimes only a single day or up to a couple of weeks for large commercials.

TVCs, and music videos are a great place to be challenged at a higher role. A 2nd AD may be the 1st AD for a commercial or a Camera Assistant may have a go at being the DOP when the opportunity arises. In this short form you can extend your skills without the pressure of an eight-week plus shoot and responsibility associated with that. The projects are often smaller and manageable for a less experienced HOD giving them the opportunity to practice their new role while still bringing their specific style and skills to the job.

Commercials are great boosters and worth your time for many reasons, but building a career on them alone won't afford you the same wide-ranging experience as a feature film or fast paced TV set. I believe working on a longer project is fundamental to establishing your skills and work ethic. There's also the reality that TV and film credits are generally more valuable on a CV than TVC credits, when going for your next big job. The exception here is for directors, where TVCs are a great place to develop and cultivate their style on short form projects and build a showreel before making a leap to a feature film or TV drama.

REALITY

Reality TV is a strange world of high rating, inexplicably bizarre shows with repetitive content and abnormal working hours. The shows can range from the vast excess of talent shows pumping out various acts to develop, to working intimately with celebrities in uncomfortable scenarios that the common human apparently finds captivating.

They are fast-paced, ratings-driven content that complement an interesting mix of control and egos. The advantages of working in reality TV is that you get to do some extraordinary things and travel to some incredible places (and be paid for it). Who wouldn't want to go to a tropical island for work or fly around the world following contestants on their loopy missions? The lifestyle can be really fun and you're guaranteed to meet a bunch of great, if not a tad eccentric, people along the way. The downside of reality is that you won't be so challenged in your storytelling ability. If you care about complex narratives or cinematography, then reality is not for you. However, it does suit people who are in it for the adventure.

I wouldn't recommend pursuing jobs in reality for an extended amount of time if you are someone who is looking to develop their skills for working in drama. Unless, of course, you score a gig with the Kardashians, who eat drama for breakfast, with kale. There are plenty of crew who specialise in reality TV, enjoying getting paid well and experiencing the wild adventure that it brings.

Ben Osmo
Sound Recordist

2015 Academy Award Winner (Best Achievement in Sound Mixing) – *Mad Max: Fury Road*

Mad Max: Fury Road, Babe, Strictly Ballroom, The Sapphires

What was your first job in the film industry?

I was a dispatch clerk at George Patterson's Advertising; I was promoted to Assistant Projectionist, and then Sound/ Video Assistant at George Patterson's video studio.

Did you study?

I studied Film Production Techniques at North Sydney Tafe. I would also say, having the opportunity of being assistant to the Sound Mixer at Kingcroft Productions, Sound Assistant at ABC Gore Hill transfer suite, and then Sound Recordist and Sound Mixer at ABC Sydney for 10 years was my education. Each project I work on is still an education, having to keep in touch with new technology in all disciplines of filmmaking including sound.

What is one piece of advice you would give to someone starting in the film industry?

Try and get an attachment or assistant position with a mentor in your area, even while on a course or after graduating. It's also good to visit other areas in filmmaking to have an overall understanding and appreciation of your industry. It'll make you a better filmmaker.

Did you think you'd be doing what you do?
I was always interested in art and music, so I fell into sound early on.

What would you be doing if you didn't work in the film industry?
Sound engineer in the music industry, singer songwriter, musician, artist, who knows?

What was your favourite job or best memory?
I can't choose just one, as there have been many great experiences so far. *Dead Calm* - five months in the Whitsunday Islands. Phillip Noyce, George Miller and Dean Semler were all inspirational. One day we were privileged to record a couple of humpback whales with a hydrophone that happened to be passing by. *Lorenzo's Oil* - was a great opportunity to work on a film in the USA. Directed by George Miller. *Strictly Ballroom* - was a challenge, using the equipment of the day (1991). We needed to record good quality 100% dialogue in incredibly challenging circumstances. *Babe* - This was another great experience. Directed by Chris Noonan and produced by Bill and George Miller, the challenge was to coordinate pre-recorded dialogue from animatronics and playback audio at different frame rates. This was so the Director could judge whether the animals' actions fitted the dialogue. *Mad Max: Fury Road* - this was a massive challenge to record. The cameras and cast were mostly on the move, travelling from 500 meters to kilometres away in various vehicles.

What's so great about the sound department?

Location sound is a craft that helps storytelling and has a close relationship with many departments. Post-production sound is a very creative craft that merges dialogue, music and effects that not only tells the story but uses psychology to influence the viewer. It's a crucial element to filmmaking and if you have an understanding of the final goal it can be fulfilling.

Why would someone pursue a career in the sound department?

If you love sound, being a recordist can be a great career. And particularly in documentaries, it can be a way to travel the world and experience life and cultures rarely seen by tourists.

How has winning an Oscar changed your career?

It's early days yet, however, funnily enough, I've just completed the location recording on a big film production – I was employed after my Oscar nomination. There have been many interviews and commitments to talk at Film Schools and Seminars for Film Guilds. An artist even painted my portrait for the Archibald prize! I have recently been given the honour to become a member of the Academy and can now vote for upcoming productions for the Oscars.

The Multitude
OF DEPARTMENTS

7

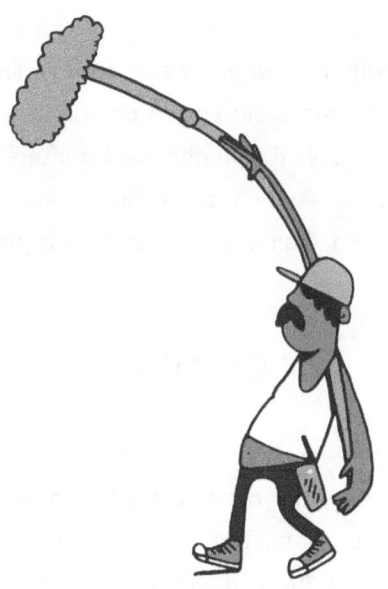

A film crew is made up of several departments; some of whom you won't even know are working on the same picture as you. Each department fulfils a specific role that combines to make the project. As evidenced by the length of credits on any modern film today, there are hundreds of people who piece together each movie. Usually there is harmony between departments, as crew often work on multiple projects together, but sometimes these connections will be tested as the project progresses and is affected by time and money constraints.

Crew members come and go through the life of the project, with the majority of people being employed for the shooting period. It's important to have a solid understanding of what all the different departments do to fully understand the process of filmmaking and to contribute to the project to your best ability. You might not be interested in every role or sometimes won't even have contact with entire departments, but their place on the film is just as valuable as your own.

ACCOUNTS

The accounts department are the magical fairies who deposit money in your bank account each week – so be on good terms with them. They look after the budget, ensure the crew and cast are paid and that invoices from suppliers are processed. They are often located in the production office with multiple accountants covering various areas of production. You will need to deal with them for all your reimbursements and petty cash, so it's a good idea to get to know them in pre-production as you may not see them a lot when you are out on location filming. They deal with everyone's account forms so make sure your forms are completed properly before submitting them to give them a helping hand and a cheerful wink.

To be in the accounts department you don't really need to have a film background. Many are accountants by trade but have an interest in film so have chosen this direction for their career. They start as a Junior Accounts Assistant and work their way up the ranks before becoming the Financial Controller, who reports to the Producer and studio regarding the financial position of the film. If you are a mathematical whizz but want to pursue a job in the film industry, this could be the perfect combination for you.

Crew Roles:
- Financial Controller
- Production Accountant
- Payroll Accountant
- Accounts Assistant

ARMOURY

By law, any prop considered to be a weapon on set needs to be held and issued by a licensed armourer. This includes actual firearms, fake firearms, handcuffs, knives, swords and anything else deemed dangerous. The Armourer abides by strict laws regarding storing and issuing these weapons on set. They will sign the item out to the appropriate cast or extra when on set and then collect the item when filming is complete, or an extended break is required. Working with the ADs and Safety Officer, the armoury team will train everyone on how to use the weapons appropriately, manage safe work practices with weapons on set and also be a wealth of knowledge for general firearm questions should you have any. Don't mess with the armourers because they have guns, lots of guns.

Crew Roles:
- Armourer
- Armoury Assistant

ANIMALS

The animals department will be very unique for each project. Some projects require simple domesticated animals like cats and dogs, while others require creatures that are rare or difficult to work with, like Pterodactyls. These animals require training, care and must be handled by observing numerous animal protection laws. Consider a film like *Evan Almighty*; they had hundreds of strange and unique animals that all needed to board the ark. I don't envy that crew. An Animal Coordinator will be employed to go through the script and work with the Director in choosing animals that will work well on set.

The trainers will spend weeks training and practising with the animals if there are specific actions they must learn. The Animal Wrangler is responsible for the safety of the crew and animals while on set and may have certain guidelines the crew must follow whilst filming the animal.

So far I have filmed kangaroos punching a cast member, maggots crawling across extras bodies, rats inhabiting underground tunnels and dogs doing various tricks they've been taught. It's always exciting having an animal on set but it can be frustrating when they won't do what they're told! As a crew member, it's important to keep quiet and calm on set when animals are present. This helps them settle and allows them to do their shot quickly so the crew can move on without too much time spent. It's great to see some rare animals on set, but be sure to check with the Animal Wrangler before patting or holding any. They don't say 'never work with kids and animals' for nothing.

Crew Roles:
- Animal Coordinator
- Animal Wrangler

ART DEPARTMENT

The art department is responsible for creating the world that the characters inhabit in the story. This may be an extremely detailed planet in outer space, or an elaborate historical city. Perhaps it is just a simple suburban home, with ordinary décor and everyday visual appeal. Without designers, set construction crew, set decorators and property buyers, this world would never exist and the story would not be able to be told in a way that immerses the audience with its believability. To achieve the vision of the Director and Production Designer, the art department may need to design and build intricate sets that are both economical in cost but also able to house a large crew, cast and extras. The set may only be used for a few days but has to appear genuine and be constructed solidly enough that a crew can work in it.

Sometimes the designers and construction crews are able to use an existing location or building and dress the space according to what the Director and Production Designer want. This may involve adding plants, changing signs, painting walls or even building in fake walls. The world of sets is often fake; timber is painted to appear as large sandstone blocks or heavy girders of a railway bridge, beautiful paintings are cheap prints that have been framed and polystyrene is used to build just about anything you can think of. The art department is so good at creating a fake world that the audience can't tell the difference.

The art department can a be a really fun crew, where you'll find yourself creating all kinds of strange worlds. This is a great department to work in if you love making things and have an eye for decorating. You can start as the Runner, or maybe even a Buyer, and work your way up the ladder to Production Designer.

Crew Roles:
- Production Designer
- Art Director
- Set Decorator
- Buyer
- Art Department Runner

ASSISTANT DIRECTORS (ADs)

The assistant director department manages the set. It is their job to balance all the parts that make up the shooting process and ensure they are all working together. This includes the cast, extras, vehicles, props, weapons, special effects and cameras. Their involvement and attention to detail takes pressure off the Director, allowing him or her to focus on the film rather than the peripheral elements. The AD Department typically consists of a 1st AD and 3rd AD on set, and a 2nd AD at unit base. As with most departments, the AD team will grow larger depending on the size of the job.

The 1st AD is responsible for creating the filming schedule in consultation with all the other HODs in pre-production. They then guide the crew as best as possible to get the project shot on time in the most efficient way. To create the shooting schedule, the 1st AD may have to take into consideration location restrictions, cast restrictions, what time of day the scene needs to shot, seasonal weather, tides and many other factors specific to each script. On set, the 1st AD manages the crew to achieve the Director's vision. They are the main point of communication for all HODs and aim to run an amicable set where everyone knows what they are shooting.

The 2nd AD spends most of their day running unit base. This begins with managing the cast and extras through makeup/hair and costume before they go in front of the camera. They then balance completing reports from the previous day of shooting, preparing tomorrow's call sheet and organising the comings and goings of cast for later scenes in the day. The 2nd AD works closely with the Production Coordinator in producing the following day's call sheet as a joint effort. The information for the call sheet is based on the 1st AD's schedule, compiled into a standard format containing all essential information for the next day of shooting.

The 2nd 2nd AD or 3rd AD is on set to assist the 1st AD in managing the cast and crew, and also to direct the extras. Working with the Director and the 1st AD, they place every background character, whether there are five or five-hundred in the scene. The Director may have strong opinions about what the background extras should be doing or may leave it entirely up to the AD's creativity. The reason the 3rd AD does this rather than the Director may be based on the limited time the boss has while doing everything else. Also, as soon as the Director actually 'directs' an extra, they receive a 'bump', which is essentially a pay rise for the day and a credit as a role in the project. To keep these costs down, the 3rd AD relays everything the Director wants and sets the background artists.

Starting out as an On-set PA (or a 3rd AD on a smaller project) is a great position to discover all the elements to film production. You will find yourself in many meetings between HODs and will be given plenty of responsibility and opportunity to test your skills. It is a demanding position with long hours and it's non-stop all day, but I would recommend trying to start with this role if you are looking to be a 1st AD or Producer.

Crew Roles:
- 1st Assistant Director
- Key 2nd Assistant Director
- 2nd 2nd Assistant Director (on and off set)
- 3rd Assistant Director
- On-set/Off-set Production Assistant

CAMERA

The camera department is responsible for all things camera-related, excluding any hardware that the cameras are placed on – dollies, cranes, sliders or any other contraption needed to mount the camera – this is done by the grips. The camera team is one of the larger departments on set, consisting of a very structured hierarchy with specific responsibilities. This team needs to be a tight-knit group, each with their individual tasks that require precision and repetition. If there is someone lacking in experience, the whole crew will notice the process slow down. The Camera Operator, 1st Assistant Camera (1st AC, also known as the Focus Puller) and 2nd Assistant Camera (2nd AC) are generally a team that has been together for multiple jobs with knowledge of exactly how each person works.

The Director of Photography (DOP) works closely with the Director and Gaffer to decide shot coverage and light the scene. They are responsible for making each and every shot beautiful and interesting. The DOP will have a rough idea of how they want the scene lit from pre-production and will now communicate this to the Gaffer and their lighting team to achieve the desired look. Even though the DOP is the camera department's HOD, often the Camera Operator or 1st AC will manage the everyday decisions of their department such as organising additional crew and equipment.

The Camera Operator frames up the shot, with guidance from the Director and DOP if needed, and communicates with other departments as to what work needs to be done in front of the lens. For example, furniture may require moving to make the space look better, equipment might be obscuring the shot, and background extras need to be directed as to what they should be doing. The Camera Operator can also double as the Steadicam Operator or a specialist Steadicam Operator may be called in on specific shoot days.

The 1st AC is responsible for making sure the camera is prepared for the Operator and focusing the lens throughout the shot. The 2nd AC assists the Operator and Focus Puller with whatever they need to make their job easier and more streamlined. This includes featuring the slate on each take, documenting camera sheet notes given to the editor along with the Script Supervisor's notes, moving all the camera gear around throughout the day, and making multiple coffees throughout the day to keep their team alive.

Depending on the size of the shoot, the camera department may also include the Video Split Operator and Digital Imaging Technician (DIT). On smaller TV and TVC jobs, the Video Split Operator will be a junior camera person running cables and moving one monitor for the Director and crew. On larger jobs, a specialised Video Split Operator will have multiple monitors for the Director, Producer, crew and visitors. They also capture all the takes to their own hard drives and are extremely useful for pulling up scenes from previous days if you need to check continuity. The DIT assists the DOP in all things 'colour' for the picture. As modern cameras capture raw files that are then manipulated through colour grade programs in post, the DIT may feed the image through an approximate colour grade or LUT (Look Up Table) on set that the DOP can view, effectively showing them close to what the final image will be. This helps them light the scene appropriately to what the finished film will look like.

Typically, people start out in the camera department if they desire to be a DOP or Camera Operator. As a junior in the camera team, it is great to start learning from experienced DOPs and technicians. You'll pick up skills by simply observing and watching them. A Clapper Loader or 2nd AC role is a great chance to get close to the action of the film set and experience the entire process. As a part of the camera team, you will work hard within a strong hierarchy, so remember to do the little things well and you will continue to learn and progress through the ranks.

Crew Roles:
- Director of Photography
- Camera Operator or Steadicam Operator
- 1st Assistant Camera (Focus Puller)
- 2nd Assistant Camera
- Clapper Loader
- Truck Loader
- Video Split Operator
- Video Split Assistant
- Digital Imaging Technician (DIT)

CAST

The cast is formed by an eclectic bunch of people of different ages, backgrounds and egos, from the 20-million-dollar-a-film types to the street-cast actors chosen purely for their 'look'. Many people chase the dream of being an actor while only a select few make a full time living out of it. It's an incredibly harsh and competitive profession that requires full commitment, and often more luck than skill. From my experience, the actors at the top of their game who are considered the best in the world are the most professional and hardworking ones. They know the script, their character, their dialogue back-to-front. They also understand filming procedures and take interest in the look the Makeup Designer and Costume Designer proposes for their character. They get the respect they deserve from the crew and often receive a positive critical reception as a result of all this hard work.

Some cast are endearing and particularly friendly with the crew, while others you'll hope to never see again. The crew does not expect to be besties with all the performers, but it is appreciated when actors learn the names of the crew and use common courtesies when on set. So to all you young superstars out there – please remember the crew is there to assist you in your performance. They will do pretty much anything you need, but it's nice to be polite about it. Your gentle manner and good attitude will speak volumes at the end of a grueling fourteen-hour day.

CASTING

The casting department is responsible for recommending actors for every role in the film. Between the Casting Director, the Director and the Producer, all the casting decisions for the film are made. A Casting Director must be up to date with what actors are considered hot right now and who is bankable. As the film can take up to a couple of years to be released, it's important they consider the projects the actor has recently done, and where this film will fit in their career with their other projects. Somebody may be considered a newcomer, but really they have three big films about to be released, so by the time this film is released, they will be a household name.

Most of the casting is outsourced to casting agencies, so the Casting Director is often never seen on a film set or in the office. The Director and Producer will have lots of initial contact with them in pre-production but once all the decisions have been made, they don't have much input in the film unless script amendments are written or someone pulls out of the project and the role needs to be recast. There are very limited Casting Director positions, so most start in extras casting or as an agent, and move into casting when their name becomes well known and they have established strong relationships with directors and producers.

Crew Roles:
- Casting Director
- Casting Assistant

CONSTRUCTION

The construction crew is tasked with the job of building the world that the Production Designer and Director design. On large films there can be up to five-hundred people working tirelessly to get sets built and finished before the shooting crew is scheduled to begin filming with them.

The construction crew has carpenters, welders, painters, engineers, sculptors and stagehands. It's amazing to see the detail to which these talented people can create while using materials that are often different to the real world. Sculptors make amazing replica stone structures out of polystyrene, carpenters and painters use cheap timber to create stone, metal and hardwood finishing, and the welders create the structure that these sets are built on that a crew of two-hundred people plus equipment can work on safely. Unfortunately, once the set has been used for filming, it serves no further purpose for the project and is stripped, dismantled and often destroyed or stored by the production company.

If you are a talented tradesperson and have an interest in working on films, the construction department is a great place to express your creative side beyond stock-standard building projects.

Crew Roles:
- Construction Manager
- Construction Foreman
- Engineer
- Carpenter
- Welder
- Painter
- Stagehand

CONTINUITY/SCRIPT SUPERVISOR

Have you ever watched a scene where the fullness of a glass keeps changing with each shot, or the scarf around the actor is up in one shot and then down in the very next? These errors can be irritating for the audience and pull them away from the suspended belief the story is aiming to create. Known either as Continuity or Script Supervisor, this crew member is a one-person department that covers all things continuity and script... as per the title.

The Script Supervisor sits with the Director and DOP and shares their expertise whenever they have questions relating to the story, where this scene fits in the storyline and continuity of items. This can be hard to track when shooting multiple scenes out of order each day, which can affect the actor's performance or emotions. The Script

Supervisor often works with the cast, assisting them with their dialogue if they are struggling to remember their lines or are saying the wrong words. As above, they keep an eye out for the continuity within scenes. E.g. How full glasses are, what hand the actor was carrying the phone in, when the background actors were cued etc., but also across the scenes for the whole project. This involves the continuity of character costumes, makeup and hair across multiple scenes.

Script Supervisors require a good memory and impeccable bookkeeping, as all the notes they make throughout the day from the Director are then passed onto the Editor to begin cutting the scenes together without the Director present. In pre-production, the Script Supervisor does a script breakdown. This involves timing each scene for an approximate run time and overall length of the film, creating story days so that every department knows the order when filming nonlinear scenes, and highlighting any particular items for the 1st AD to work into their schedule.

The Script Supervisor is an integral part of any film process, but often gets overlooked in low budget features or short films. This is concerning as it is typically an invaluable resource to the Director, cast and Editor in ensuring any potential inaccuracies are removed before progressing to the edit.

COSTUME

The costume department designs, buys, sews and tailors costumes for the film to create a specific look and colour tone for each character and scene. After the initial designs have been drawn, the costume team then goes about buying, making and adjusting costumes to fit each character. Some costumes can be easily bought or hired, while others are made from scratch by skilled seamstresses. Every project will have different costumes depending on the context of the film. E.g. An 1800's period piece set in London, compared to a sci-fi set in 2087.

Extras in the film also need costumes to reflect the magical world of the film. There can be up to five-hundred background extras at one time in large scenes. To achieve this, the costume department will have a large warehouse with hundreds of racks of clothing. Each extra will be called in for a fitting and dressed according to their shape, and the style the Costume Designer chooses. It is a massive process to fit and tailor everyone for the film, and takes up many weeks of pre-production, often continuing as the crew begins to shoot. In pre-production, the costume workrooms are a hive of activity. As the film goes into production and the majority of costumes have been completed, the workroom will slow in production and focus on the priorities of supporting the set as filming takes place.

The costume department is perfect for all those personal stylists among you. There are different types of roles split between the costume workroom where the clothes are sewn and fitted, and the on-set standbys who deal with any mishaps that occur on set, such as lost buttons or split pants. The costume department is a favourable department to crack into, with many positions available in pre-production. If you possess the skills of sewing, leatherwork, or millinery craft, you'll be a great asset to this fashion-savvy team. To get your foot in the door, you can start as a Runner/Buyer, or even in the workroom creating costumes. Once again, it's usually a case of who you know that will nab you that first opportunity.

Crew Roles:
- Costume Designer
- Costume Supervisor
- Costume Standby
- Extras Costume Supervisor
- Extras Costume Standby
- Seamstress
- Costume Buyer
- Costume Runner

DIRECTOR

The Director is the boss on set, or as one 1st AD I know calls them, the 'El Presidente'. Essentially all the departments are working to achieve the Director's vision. The Producer typically appoints the Director to steer the project in the path they deem appropriate and they duly receive the respect and support they deserve for carrying the film. It's not often people will say 'no' to their boss, especially to an experienced and well respected one. At times, a crew might need to say, 'We'll see what we can do' as a lenient alternative to cutting off the requests of their Director, but rarely is 'no' an option.

Your relationship with the Director will be different depending on what department you are in. You may have lots to do with them in pre-production but little during the shoot, or maybe even very little altogether except for the fact you are helping to create their vision. It's good to get to know them when appropriate so they can rely on you for what they need. It's very easy to become cynical and criticise some directors, particularly after a few years in the industry, as it can be a very demanding job and sometimes a young or inexperienced Director is still finding their way. The crew expects to be led with all the wisdom and life experience of Yoda, but sometimes end up with more of a Ja Ja Binx. Every Director works in his/her own style and it is important to nurture and encourage that creativity rather than criticise them for not doing it your way.

The Director may also be the scriptwriter, or may have been employed by the Producer purely for directing this film. Either way will give the project a distinctive feel. Writer/ directors will be particularly focused on the story they have already slaved over for years, while non-writing directors may be able to cope with story changes without flinching, as it isn't their personal work.

There are many different paths young filmmakers can take to becoming a Director, and everyone will have a different opinion on how to get there. You could start out working as an Assistant Editor to perfect the art of assembling takes and knowing what is needed to cover a scene. Or, if you're a writing whiz, you might pen a few features and aim to get them bought before trying to direct your first feature. You might start out directing short films and music videos to identify your style and build a showreel that a Producer may like before poaching you for a feature or TV episode. Whatever way you chase the dream is entirely your choice and the experiences and lessons you learn along the way will prove invaluable for that incredible moment when you direct a $200 million blockbuster.

EXTRAS

Extras, or background artists, create the surrounding world of people who inhabit the set. They are all the characters in a scene who don't have dialogue. Extras are an integral piece of nearly every scene: creating large armies, bustling cities and populating various workspaces. The ADs are responsible for directing the extras, as well as making sure they know what to do and where to be on set. This can be simple with only a few people in the scene or can take a large team with hundreds of extras spread over a massive set.

Extras can be pursuing acting careers, be interested in jobs in the film industry or may just want a bit of cash and fun on the side. The majority of extra work is quite easy as you are told exactly what to do, get fed breakfast, lunch and afternoon tea, and get to go off set and sit down whenever you aren't being used. However, recently I worked on a war film and the soldier extras were worked to the absolute bone. They were used in almost every shot and the terrain and conditions were extremely demanding. They had a great time though, and built a strong sense of camaraderie throughout the shoot as everyone looked out for one another.

The crew can often get frustrated with the behaviour of extras as they may not know set etiquette, and larger groups can become a nuisance to work around if they are not directed properly. As a result of this, I think extras get a bad rap for being 'daft' or considered the lowest in the film industry. Like any job, sometimes there are bad eggs and I have dealt with them first hand, but the majority of extras are lovely people giving everything they have to their job and wanting to be as professional as the rest of the crew.

If you really can't find any way of getting some experience on set, joining an extras agency may be a good idea. It should be free to sign up as they usually take 10% of your earnings rather than an initial fee. This will give you on-set experience from this perspective and hopefully you'll be able to meet some people who can point you in the right direction or take you on for work experience. You'll also make a bit of money and get fed really well while you learn a few things about what happens on set.

EXTRAS CASTING

The extras casting department are responsible for casting all the background roles for the film. This can be an epic scene of huge crowds on larger films but is usually around thirty to fifty people on average days. The Extras Casting Director works closely with the Director and Producer in pre-production to decide on the look they want for each scene. They trawl through thousands of photos of people from extras agencies to find a specific look and range of people. For modern dramas this may be as easy as replicating a contemporary suburban scene, but many scenes require particular people to make the world look genuine and exactly as the Director wants. Once chosen, extras are fitted with a costume, given a haircut if needed and booked for their scheduled days on the film. An experienced Extras Casting Director can provide the Director with individuals that match the exact look they are after for the scene as well as picking a bunch of people that perform well on camera and work well with the ADs.

Extras are a diverse bunch – some work an extra full time gig on the road to stardom, while others are there to earn some additional cash and see how films are made. This can present all kinds of challenges for the Extras Casting Director and ADs as film sets are unique work environments and they need to ensure everyone is safe while also achieving the Director's vision. Over time, the ADs will get to know the regular extras and will build a relationship of trust and reliance with the experienced ones.

Crew Roles:
- Extras Casting Director
- Extras Casting Assistant

GRIPS

The grips are the Meccano and Lego experts you always envied as a kid. They can build anything from the kit in their truck, and are the muscle of the film set. The main purpose of the grips is to build any hardware for the camera to be placed on. This can include dolly tracks, camera cranes, scaffold towers, car mounts and tracking vehicles. The grips are generally very experienced film technicians, having spent years under the tutelage of their superiors before either starting their own grip company or becoming a Key Grip. It is important for the grips to be great at their job not only from a speed perspective, as some of the builds can take multiple hours, but also from a safety perspective. The rigs they build need to be safe to hold the camera so it will not fall off and break the expensive equipment or injure someone.

If you need something done that involves muscle on set, the grips will generally be willing to lend a hand, especially if you ask politely and at the right time. If you need something built they will most likely have an appropriate tool and equipment in their truck, and given the right amount of time, are often willing to help and take you on as an apprentice. On each new job the grips are generally testing out their latest new toy, whether it be a fancy new electric vehicle or a camera crane. They love their toys and are happy to show them to you but remember, don't touch!

To start out as a Grip you will be the Truck Loader or Junior Grip. You won't spend much time on set but will look after the truck and gear dump, racing to set any specifically named piece of equipment your seniors call for. This is how you learn what everything is called and what it is used for. You will get opportunities every now and again to help build rigs when things are busy on set. On larger films, a Junior Grip will get to experience all the cool pieces of equipment like cranes and tracking vehicles but won't get as much hands-on experience as you would on a smaller TV show with a team of three or four. Most young grips go between large and small projects to get a holistic understanding of their department and what is needed.

Crew Roles:

- Key Grip
- Best Boy Grip
- Dolly Grip
- Grip
- Assistant Grip
- Junior Grip/Truck Loader

LIGHTING

The lighting technicians are like a god on any set, as they create the light. Well, at least they sometimes think they are. Lighting sets the lamps under the guidance of the Gaffer and DOP, and also provides power for the entire set from their generator. Every scene requires different lighting to create certain moods, and so they have a variety of equipment to achieve the desired look. Sometimes they will simply utilise natural sunlight with no equipment necessary, but when the clouds roll in, they may use large 20K lamps to replicate the sunlight that is now blocked.

The lighting crew will grow depending upon the size of the job, with normally four technicians for TV shows and up to fifteen technicians for large films. When shooting on the sound stages, there will also be a separate crew of lighting technicians known as rigging electrics. This crew prepares any lighting on the grid above and in the sets that can be pre-set before the shooting crew starts. This saves a lot of time, so the Gaffer can then make any tweaks with their on-set crew to achieve the desired look of the DOP.

If you need power for any of your electronics on set such as chargers or monitors, it is important to double check with one of the lighting crew whether it's okay to plug into their distribution board or into house power. This is to ensure you don't overload their circuits or trip any circuit breakers. They can also provide power cables, power boards and work lights if you ask nicely.

Starting out in the lighting department is a great place for people that want to learn about lighting scenes. This is terrific for aspiring DOPs or Gaffers. Be prepared to work hard as the lighting technicians run cables all around set and are constantly racing the clock to get every lamp set before cameras need to roll.

Crew Roles:
- Gaffer
- Best Boy Electrics
- Lighting Technician
- Rigging Gaffer
- Rigging Best Boy
- Rigging Technician

LOCATIONS

The location department looks after all the locations of a film shoot. It sounds fairly obvious on first observation – but how do you shoot a script set in 1920s New York – in 21st century Sydney? A film desperately requires savvy location scouts to discover some of the most obscure locations that can be transformed into amazing sets to capture the story.

During pre-production, the Location Manager and Location Scout break down the script and search for appropriate places to film. This could be nature reserves, cityscapes, houses, beaches, tourist icons, railways and gardens - pretty much anywhere someone can think to write about. After a location has been found and the Director is happy with the look of the place, the Location Manager will then work with the various governing bodies or owners to negotiate fees, dates and infrastructure for the crew to film there. Location managers have to juggle relationships with councils, property owners, national park regulators, traffic authorities plus the demands of the film crew to ensure everybody is satisfied during the shoot. Owners can be particularly difficult to work with as they might initially be enticed by the amount of money offered to use their property, but when they see two-hundred crew members and equipment stomping all over their precious house and gardens, they may have second thoughts or even back out. The Location Manager needs to placate the owner while ensuring the crew are respecting the property and not causing any damage.

Film crews can go to very remote locations without power, water and other facilities. The Location Manager works closely with the Unit Manager and Production Manager to provide the services needed for filming to take place in that particular area. They are responsible for all paperwork and permits for locations and juggle the locations budget with the approval of the Producer and Production Manager.

Starting out in the locations department can be an ideal way to see both sides of filmmaking, as you get to spend time in the office and on set. There aren't too many location department positions going around, but a good place to start is to help out with student films or short films, as even they need places scouted and permissions granted. You can then slowly build up a portfolio of locations you have used. To be a Location Manager you need to be a skilled negotiator and be super people-oriented. They can generally talk themselves out of a hostage crisis and distract people long enough for filming to take place. If you see somewhere, or something interesting in your travels or everyday life, take a photo and write down the address – you never know when you'll read a script and have the perfect waterfall or art deco apartment block you can recommend.

When my work experience was organised during my study, I was originally assigned to the locations department.

I arrived at the office bright-eyed on day one, but the Location Manager suggested I'd have a much better time if I was on set with the ADs because they were midway through the shoot and most of the interesting locations work had already been completed. He drove me to set, introduced me, and I've been working as an AD ever since. Life, right?

Crew Roles:
- Location Manager
- Location Scout
- Location Assistant

MAKEUP/HAIR ARTIST

The makeup and hair department are the early risers of the crew, with call times well before the sun comes up to get the cast ready for when shooting begins. The makeup artists transform the cast into their characters based on a brief by the Director and Makeup Designer. This may oscillate anywhere from a simple, natural look with minimal makeup, to a transformative alien character with prosthetics, to a terrifyingly bloodied and maimed zombie. In pre-production, the cast may have their hair dyed, trimmed, extensions put in, beards grown, fake tattoos applied, prosthetics fitted, contacts made – anything that makes them look genuine as their character. After the cast has been made up, the makeup artists then travel to set with their respective cast member to apply any touch ups as necessary throughout the day.

Makeup artists typically go to a makeup school before attaching to a film as a work experience student or Junior Makeup Artist. Many makeup artists specialise in different areas like hairdressing or prosthetics, with the Makeup Designer building a team that suits the jobs requirements depending on the script and characters.

Crew Roles:
- Makeup Designer
- Key Makeup Artist
- Wig Mistress
- Makeup Artist
- Hair Artist

MARINE

The marine department handles all transport and safety that takes place on water. This will range from simply getting crew from one place to another on a hired ferry, to creating a pontoon city in the ocean when filming scenes at sea. Water scenes will often be executed in large tanks at the studio, but occasionally the project requires open water filming, creating a bunch of logistical issues the marine department needs to navigate. Not only do they need to prepare correct vessels for filming to take place, they also need to manage the crew's safe travel and work whilst at sea.

The marine team also has safety divers in case anything goes wrong, or something (or someone...) is dropped into the water. The divers are also present whenever a cast or crew member is in the water for filming purposes to assist them and also oversee safety. Marine teams are quite rare on films as it's a very specific department, but when they are required, they need to be the best in the business, as managing conditions on the ocean can be challenging with one boat, let alone fifteen to twenty when a large film crew is involved. Working on water always makes things harder and slower so it's important that the marine department supplies the appropriate equipment so the production is not hindered and everyone is kept safe.

Crew Roles:
- Marine Coordinator
- Boat Driver
- Dive Master
- Safety Diver

PICTURE VEHICLES

Not to be confused with the transport department, the picture vehicles department handles any vehicle that is used on camera. This can be standard cars, military vehicles, boats, trucks, motorcycles and anything else the Director can dream up that can be built and driven. Sometimes this department is absorbed into the art department on smaller jobs, but on jobs where unique or many vehicles are required, there will be a separate department to oversee this. These crew members generally have a mechanical background so they can fix any issues that may arise while filming. This can be particularly difficult when you are using cars that are sixty or seventy years old in some period projects, or have been completely custom made just for the project. They are also welders, machinists and fabricators that build and modify various vehicles.

On *Mad Max: Fury Road*, the vehicles department spent years and years designing, building, testing and modifying all the crazy vehicles that George Miller and his design team could think up. The vehicles were shipped from Australia to Namibia, to be used in the amazing desert landscapes. Throughout the film, most of the vehicles were crashed, blown up or destroyed as part of the action. Essentially, the vehicles team were employed to build amazingly unique vehicles, before watching them be annihilated in front of their eyes.

As an actor may be required to drive a car in shot, the vehicles department also helps the cast familiarise themselves with it, giving them test drives and coaching before filming takes place. This makes the actor comfortable driving the vehicle in the scene while they are in character. It's also a good test to make sure they will be safe around the crew on set, and not endanger anyone else who has to be in or near the vehicle. If the cast member is deemed not suitable to drive, a stunt double will be dressed and used for the driving scenes where necessary, or simulated travel will be used to complete the driving shots.

Picture vehicle departments come and go with many having mechanical jobs outside of the industry, but when a once-in-a-lifetime experience like *Mad Max: Fury Road* comes along, everyone jumps at the opportunity to display their skills and be part of an impressively crazy film.

Crew Roles:
- Vehicle Coordinator
- Assistant Vehicle Coordinator
- Picture Vehicle Driver

POST-PRODUCTION

The post-production team has the mountainous job of distilling all that was shot and compiling it into the polished final cut for the screen. This includes managing the edit, sound edit, soundtrack, titles and working with the visual effects team to add in their work. I've heard from one Director that the final product is never as good as your rushes but never as bad as the rough cut.

As soon as day one of filming is complete, the Editor will start to receive footage and work on piecing together the project. They will complete assemblies for the Director and Producer to view as filming continues. The Editor will use the Script Supervisor's notes and input from the Director where available, but will cut everything together as they see fit. Once principal photography has wrapped, the Editor and Director will spend days and days together fine-tuning every little cut. The job is arduous and will test everyone's patience, but is worth the effort having just spent so much time filming. The sign of a great Editor is one who saves time and also suggests ideas the Director may not have even considered, enhancing the film with their expertise.

After the edit is locked, the sound team will create a sound mix while a soundtrack is scored, titles are designed, and the Colourist will do their grade with the supervision of the DOP. Usually, post-production takes three to four times the shoot length, as many weeks are spent finessing the final cut. Many people don't realise the work involved after a project has been shot and question why it takes so long to be released after filming has completed. Well, now you know!

There are numerous roles on offer in post-production, with new jobs being added as technologies advance and change. Pursuing a position as a Junior Editor can be a beneficial place for aspiring directors to begin as it gives an insight into how edits come together and the coverage needed for scenes to work. You may not get much experience on set in post-production, but you do get an overall view of what it takes to complete a project and the sometimes seemingly unending challenges that will arise throughout the editing process.

Crew Roles:

- Post-production Supervisor
- Editor
- Assistant Editor
- Colourist
- Sound Designer
- Composer
- Post-production Assistant
- Post-production Runner

PRODUCTION OFFICE

The production office comprises crew members ranging from the Producer of the project through to the multitude of runners and PAs that keep things moving throughout the shoot. This office is generally one of the largest departments and is the central hub of any project. It is led by the Unit Production Manager (UPM) and/or Line Producer who manage the everyday running of the film as a representative for the Producer. They work closely with the Producer to ensure the budget is being adhered to with each decision but are given the responsibility of managing the crew on behalf of the Producer. The UPM and Line Producer will balance their time between the office in meetings and being on set to deal with any issues that arise throughout the shoot. Apart from specific tasks and responsibilities of each individual's role, the production office is responsible for issuing scripts, schedules, memos and the daily call sheet to ensure the crew is aware of what is happening.

Communication to the production office should go through the Production Coordinator and/or Production Secretary if departments need things purchased, additional crew booked or other issues relating directly to production of the film. As with the other departments, the size and structure of the office will change depending on the specifics of the project but there are always common positions and procedures that are followed. It's important to foster a good relationship with these crew members, particularly the UPM, as it's very likely you will be dealing with them on future projects. Remember that they are dealing with the entire shooting crew so sometimes things may take slightly longer than expected.

The production office is a great place to start your film career if you are interested in producing or production managing. It's a hive of activity throughout the entire shoot, dealing with any unforeseen circumstances as they pop up. It's important to have a great attention to detail and willingness to go the extra mile even if it's not asked of you, but this applies to almost every role in the film industry. Many crew members start their careers as runners in the office. This is because it's the most junior role you can get and the turnover of runners is high as they move onto new positions after a few projects. A Runner is a perfect role to begin with as you have little responsibility, get to meet the entire crew and see both sides of production. I know a 1st Assistant Director who started as a Runner on a big film franchise and ended up as the 1st AD on that same franchise many years later. If you are looking to get your foot in the door as a Runner, email a bunch of production managers and production coordinators and hopefully in the next little while, someone will have a project you can start on.

Crew Roles:
- Producer
- Executive Producer
- Line Producer
- Production Manager
- Production Coordinator
- Assistant Production Coordinator
- Production Secretary
- Office Production Assistant
- Runner

PROPERTY

The property or 'props' department is a sub-department of the art department, responsible for all the props that are used in the film. This includes mobile phones, food and drinks, cigarettes, handbags, stationery – pretty much anything specific to the story and era that the cast and extras carry or interact with on the set. The standby props team will issue and collect props from the cast and extras for each scene to create a more realistic environment.

The property department is required to pay special attention to the order of scenes and the props that are used throughout the storyline to ensure continuity is maintained. They also need to be prepared with doubles of important items in case they break or are lost during filming.

An Assistant Standby Props role is a great way to start in this department if that is what you are interested in. You will get valuable experience on set, as well as seeing the broader roles of the art department at work throughout the shoot. MacGyver skills are a must for this department as you will be required to mock up makeshift props or repair problems on the run with whatever you can get your hands on.

Crew Roles:
- Property Master
- Props Buyer
- Standby Props
- Assistant Standby Props

PUBLICITY

Each project requires a Publicist to manage all the media coverage that goes along with a film being shot and released. The publicity is usually outsourced to a specialised Publicist who handles the Electronic Press Kit (EPK), media interviews, news stories and other publicity opportunities for the project. They report to the Producer and studio after devising a plan that is best suited to marketing the project. The publicist will come and go from the set as needed, sometimes balancing multiple projects at a time.

Crew Roles:
- Unit Publicist
- EPK Camera Operator
- EPK Sound Recordist

SAFETY/MEDIC

The safety and medic department ensures that safe work practices are followed and treat any illness or injury on set. Different productions adhere to various workplace safety laws but often a Safety Supervisor is present on set to ensure all crew members are working in a safe environment and following appropriate procedures and guidelines. Film crews have to deal with many safety issues including extreme weather, special effects, working at heights, working in confined spaces and working alongside large machinery. The set is fast-paced with many crew working to exhaustion, so it's important that someone is concerned with the safety and welfare of the crew. You'll be grateful for these guys, trust me!

The medic team will usually consist of a nurse who looks after the health of the crew and deals with any minor injuries that occur on set. On dangerous days where large stunts or special effects are involved, a paramedic and ambulance will be called in on standby in case anything goes wrong. The medic team is prepared to deal with anything from small cuts to broken bones and everything in between. They aim to keep the crew fit and healthy so that everybody makes it through the shoot alive and kicking. By law, a nurse is also required when children or babies are on set to ensure they are looked after and that the schedule will not negatively affect the wellbeing of the young child.

Drugs and alcohol will not be tolerated on set. The unspoken rule is that no one abuses any substance that could lead to someone else's injury or death. If anyone is suspected of being under the influence of drugs or alcohol they will be sent home and the Producer will determine appropriate actions.

Crew Roles:
- Safety Supervisor
- Nurse

SOUND

The sound department is a fairly small department recording all the dialogue and sound of the scenes on set. The sound team can be as small as just a singular Sound Recordist, but more often constitutes a Recordist, Boom Operator and a Sound Assistant. The Recordist captures the sound of a scene to a device other than the camera, which is synced to the picture in post-production and edited accordingly. Unwanted sounds are removed and sound effects can be added in post but it is vital to have a good sound recording during filming in order to make post-production as easy as possible.

The Boom Operator holds a long pole, known as a boom, with a microphone attached to the end. They hold this as close as possible to the actors but just out of frame to get the best sound recording. If you choose to be a Boom Operator you need to be able to hold your arms up for the duration of the scene, sometimes four or five minutes. Who'd want to do that!? You'd likely require two tickets to the gun show. The Sound Assistant attaches radio microphones under the actor's costumes as a backup to the boom microphone.

As this is such a small department, sound can be hard to crack into, as there aren't many opportunities available. You may get lucky and fall into an opening but if this is what you want to pursue, it may be a good idea to do some work at a post-sound edit facility to begin with. Here you will get an overview of the audio side of filmmaking and will develop important relationships with sound recordists. As opportunities become available, you will hear about them and already be trained to fill the position.

Crew Roles:
- Sound Recordist
- Boom Operator
- Sound Assistant

SPECIAL EFFECTS (SFX)

Special effects (SFX) include smoke, rain, water, snow, wind, steam, fire, gimbals, simulated travel, pyrotechnics, breakaways, and anything else the Director can think of that this highly skilled department can build and operate. The SFX department consists of engineers, welders, metal workers, pyro technicians, carpenters and other skilled professionals to design and build rigs that are specific to the script. They are generally split into two crews: a team residing in a large workshop where the rigs are designed and built, and the on-set technicians who operate the rigs and create the effects whilst filming.

The department will spend pre-production building any contraptions they need for certain scenes, and will be present on set when these elements are being used. This can be mechanical gimbals for simulated car or boat travel, remote control props such as Jack Sparrow's compass in *Pirates of the Caribbean*, building working streams, waterfalls and pools into the sets, and prepping vehicles or sets that explode or catch fire. The opportunities are endless for the SFX department and often if something is difficult to build and operate, it will be handballed to this department. They test and test and test so nothing can go wrong and no time is wasted during the shoot period. Still, the unexpected can happen, but the technicians work as quickly as possible to repair or modify the apparatus to continue filming. On large action films there is a sizeable team of SFX crew with many days involving these SFX elements, but on smaller drama films they may only be required for a few days throughout the shoot for rain, wind or other simple effects.

The SFX department is a dangerous one, as they are often working with fire, pyrotechnics, moving rigs and large machines. They need to ensure that they are safe while operating and also that the cast and crew will not be injured under any circumstance. The SFX crew will have specific tickets and licenses to operate all the varying machinery, and are extremely skilled in their specific roles. It's actually quite amazing what you see them build and operate, and the timeframe that they can achieve it in. They are also extremely handy if you ever need an item repaired or can't get something to work. With their truck designed like a travelling hardware store, they usually have something to help you out.

The SFX department is definitely one of the 'cooler' departments to be a part of, because they have swagger and general pyro vibes, but you will require all sorts of safety tickets to get involved. Usually, they each specialise in a certain area and are responsible for that one thing over the course of the shoot. This may be a set piece on a gimbal or the explosions that take place in various scenes. If you like making things explode, are handy on the tools and machines or love building interesting rigs, you'll fit right in the wild world of special effects. Otherwise, perhaps something else might suit you better.

Crew Roles:
- SFX Supervisor
- Workshop Supervisor
- On-set SFX Supervisor
- SFX Technician

STAND-INS

Stand-ins, or 'second team', are used to frame up each shot, set the lighting and rehearse camera moves without the actors present. Each stand-in represents one of the characters in the shot, and walks through the actions mimicking what the actor will do in the takes. The reason stand-ins are used is because lighting and rehearsing shots can sometimes take upwards of an hour. It's a waste of time for the actors to be doing all this when their time can be best used getting their makeup applied, putting on their costume or discussing the scene with the Director. It is also exhausting for the cast to do all these rehearsals before delivering their performance, so by using stand-ins you save the cast's best performances for when the cameras are rolling. The ADs, Camera Operator, DOP and Gaffer will use the second team to rehearse the scene over and over until everything is right to shoot. The cast will then be invited to set with everyone ready to roll. The stand-ins will often show the cast where their marks are and what they have rehearsed with the camera team when they arrive on set.

Each stand-in will be of similar height, weight, skin tone and hair colour to the actor they are representing, so they are mimicking what the actor will be doing in the takes to the best of their ability. Stand-ins are generally inexperienced actors looking to gain more experience and thus can do everything the actor will but can't quite nail the performances yet. Not all shows use stand-ins as it's an added cost to production that some budgets do not allow for. However, all big name stars will ensure they have one on films to take pressure off themselves, and some even travel with a personal stand-in who does all their projects with them.

A stand-in can be a great role for amateur actors trying to get more on-set experience as you will be right amongst the action, dealing with many departments and the Director. You will also learn a lot of tips from the ADs, Camera Operators and Director that will help your acting career along the way.

To be a good stand-in, it's important that you are always on time as you are usually the first person used at crew call to block out the scene. As an AD, one of the first things to do when I arrive on set is to make sure the stand-ins are ready to go for the scene. You will need a good memory to watch what the actor does and then mimic it when they step off and you line up the next shot. Don't talk too much as you need to be listening for direction and it's distracting for everyone if the stand-in won't stay still or hold their eyeline. It can feel a bit awkward to stare at someone for twenty minutes at a time, but this is necessary while the camera and lighting department do their work around you. It seems like a simple job to do – be on time, listen, remember and stare at someone for extended periods, but a proactive and skilful stand-in will help almost all departments and save time for production along the shoot.

Getting cast as a stand-in is a bit of luck because you need to be of similar size and appearance as the actor. Extras casting will pick out potential candidates from their photos and measurements and offer them as options to the ADs. They may have a trial period or the ADs may have worked with them already and know their skill level. Sometimes, the Director will get to know the stand-in along the course of the shoot and love their hard work so will reward them with a bit part of a few lines in a scene. The harder you work, the greater your chances of exposure.

STILLS PHOTOGRAPHER

The Stills Photographer comes and goes throughout a shoot, capturing important scenes or events for publicity purposes. They aim to take a variety of shots, including production stills, behind-the-scenes and the poster shot, all for use in media outlets as the film is promoted and released. An experienced film photographer can discern when to capture, expertly balancing both the cast and the filming that is taking place. They don't want to be a distraction or irritation, but they do have a brief of images they need to capture throughout the day and so this is their prerogative. Professional stills photographers will have noise cancelling camera cases known as blimps, to allow them to shoot during takes without the noise of their shutters interrupting the sound being recorded.

STUNTS

The stunt department is made up of fearless Evel Knievel imitators who do all the dangerous manoeuvres on screen that the actors can't perform. Forget what you hear on Ellen or Late Night shows when actors claim they do all their own stunts – they are clearly still acting because it's a falsity.

Stunt performers can be cast with a particular role to perform a car crash or fight scene, as a stunt double to one of the main actors, or as a crowd stunt performer for large scenes that require lots of stunties. Often, stunt performers will double up roles and play multiple parts on the film, as there are limited stunt performers available, and they are usually unrecognisable in full costume. Stunt doubles will be of similar build and look to the cast member they are doubling for and are used for anything deemed too dangerous or requiring specialised skills beyond that of the actor. The actor will perform all the safe takes and dialogue before the stunt double will take over and perform the dangerous portion of the action.

The Stunt Coordinator works with the Director to ensure that what they are asking for can be performed safely and will look good on camera. The Director often defers to the Stunt Coordinator in action sequences, as they are the most experienced for these situations. The stunt team will choreograph and rehearse the stunts before the shoot day to ensure it looks perfect and is safe to perform. The risk increases if the elements are changed on set compared to what was rehearsed or discussed, but with the guidance of the Stunt Coordinator, the action may be adjusted to look better on camera or for the Director.

Stunt people train frequently and consistently, and require stunt certification to be classified as a stunt performer. If you'd classify yourself as someone bouncing off the walls and grew up practicing wrestling choke slams on your little brother, then this could be your sweet spot. You can sign up to a stunt gym to start learning, or just practice rolling cars in your paddock like some crazy people I know. The career of a stunt performer is relatively short due to the high amount of injuries and toll on the body this work takes. The paycheck can be amazing for those at the top level receiving large stunt loadings and residuals on top of their daily wages. Often stunt performers will perform for ten to fifteen years before becoming a Stunt Coordinator, Stunt

Rigger or Safety Officer. This way they can extend their career without completely destroying their body.

Crew Roles:
- Stunt Coordinator
- Assistant Stunt Coordinator
- Stunt Rigger
- Stunt Assistant
- Stunt Double
- Stunt Performer

TRANSPORT

The transport department is tasked with driving the cast (and sometimes the crew) to and from set. Not all productions have transport departments, but as the budget and size of the project grows, it becomes a crucial department. They also move the equipment trucks and green rooms on larger jobs from location to location – this is known as the swing gang. It can involve bumping thirty to forty trucks from one location to another hours away overnight, and having it setup for the crew to shoot there the next day. Large films come with incredible infrastructure and the transport department ensures it is all there and working for the crew at each location.

Being a driver can be a simple way to work on the larger films. There are many roles available and you will get a chance to spend time with the cast or potentially the

Director, Producer and the like. As long as you have a licence and good driving skills, there will be plenty of opportunities for work in the transport department. Often people will choose to do a few jobs in the transport department if they are young writers and directors as it's a way to keep your foot in the door without much responsibility. Transport is a much easier department to crack into than, say, the camera department or as an assistant director, but can also lead to good opportunities when you meet the right people. You will get the chance to meet other crew members and hopefully create a relationship that may get you future jobs in departments you are most interested in.

Crew Roles:
- Transport Captain
- Transport Coordinator
- Driver
- Swing Gang

UNIT

The unit department is probably the most underappreciated department in film production, pulling the longest hours of the entire crew. They are usually the first people to arrive and the last to leave. They manage unit base, the essential vehicle parking, crew parking, crew toilets, tea and coffee, and everything in between. The Unit Manager works with the Location Manager, Production Manager and Transport Manager to ensure there is ample parking and facilities at the shooting location, and a suitable space for unit base where the crew will have makeup/costume trucks, green rooms, catering and crew parking.

Racking up long hours and extremely early starts takes its toll throughout a shoot, so the unit department is only for those prepared to be red-eyed and sleep deprived. Personally, starting out in the unit department isn't my cup of tea. Maybe I'm too scared of getting my hands dirty, but pumping portaloos and driving trucks around the set at all hours of the day isn't my dream job. Some, though, love the hard work and money that can be earned from all the overtime. In the unit department, the start and end of the day is busy with setup and pack up but things slow down in the middle of the day as the crew is settled and gets into the rhythm of filming.

If the unit department sounds like something you'd be interested in, I'd advise you to get your truck licence and a slab of Red Bull. For everyone else, make sure you get to know the unit department as I guarantee, before too long, they will be doing a favour for you.

Crew Roles:
- Unit Manager
- Assistant Unit Manager
- Unit Assistant

VISUAL EFFECTS (VFX)

Visual effects (VFX) refer to computer-generated graphics that are added to each scene in post-production. This can be as simple as adding some clouds to a blue sky or as in-depth as creating a complete environment behind a scene that was shot against a green or blue screen. Visual effects are becoming more and more popular as technology advances and images become more true to life. These days, visual effects can include makeup and prosthetics added to characters, entire cities and landscapes, imagined animals and characters or in the case of an animated film – literally everything! The VFX department is also responsible for removing any unwanted items in shot such as cast stunt wires, crew that were necessary to be in shot for safety reasons, equipment that was either there for a reason or sometimes accidentally left in shot, and any unwanted buildings or landscape features.

The VFX Supervisor is always present on set, working with the Director and Camera Operator, as they position cameras and frame shots. As they regularly have specific ideas to make the real life action and visual effect world seamlessly integrate, they will often put forward suggestions for shots or even sometimes take over from the Director in setting up a shot if it requires lots of VFX elements.

The size of the VFX department will be proportional to the nature of the film. An animated feature will have hundreds of visual effect artists working for years on various elements of the film, whereas a modern drama film may only have a few visual effects crew for any simple effects needed. The majority of the VFX department are off-set and employed during post-production, although there will be a small crew on set capturing data and camera information during the shoot to assist with the post-production process. This includes filming a metallic silver ball at the completion of a camera setup. The ball has a shiny side and a matte side to reflect all the light sources used in the scene that will then be replicated when the visual effects are added. This tool gets a very technical term, 'Balls', and is held where the subject of the scene was and any camera moves are replicated. Trust me, you'll be calling out 'Balls!' with the rest of the crew before you know it – it's a unanimous crew 'favourite moment'.

If you consider yourself an avid computer geek and want to start out in the world of visual effects, you are best off pursuing one of the many visual effects houses for junior roles. There are hundreds of jobs for large VFX heavy feature films but the work is contractual and seasonal. This is similar to any on-set position, and once you have a good reputation, you can bounce from project to project with minimal downtime. Usually, productions will contract out portions of the film to various VFX production houses around the country, and even around the world, with many different companies all working on the same film. They may specialise in a certain effect but often the reason is due to the amount of work and the turnaround time of the film.

Crew Roles:
- VFX Producer
- VFX Supervisor
- VFX Data Wrangler
- VFX Artists

WRITERS

The Writer creates the script for the Director and Producer to work from. This can be an original screenplay, a book adapted for film or a series of scripts for a TV show. Sometimes the Writer is also the Director or Producer, or they could be employed by the Producer to pen a script on an idea they have, or from a book they own the rights to.

Most of the writer's work is done years before the film goes into production, with many drafts completed before filming starts. It's not uncommon for amendments to be written during production, with last minute character changes and developments added. Sometimes the Writer may change as the project goes through development, as one writer might complete the original screenplay before a new one comes on board for additional changes closer to the shooting dates.

The life of a Writer can be a tough one, spending years honing skills and trying to sell work. I personally believe writers are undervalued and underappreciated, as this is where the story and characters are developed, which can determine from the very start whether the project is unique or is headed to be a flop. Often, writers are left to themselves to develop their careers as it's a very personal profession but I believe producers, directors and studios can all benefit from developing the skills of a young writer.

If you are a young writer, the best thing you can do is simple – keep writing. The more scripts you churn out, the better you will become, and hopefully one day someone will appreciate your skill and buy one/many of your scripts. Keep going!

PJ Voeten
1st Assistant Director

Mad Max: Fury Road, The Great Wall, Hacksaw Ridge,
Happy Feet

What was your first job in the film industry?

My first job was with an equipment rental company called Samuelsons. They were the agent for Panavision and initially I worked downstairs in the lighting equipment department. Eventually I decided that I wanted to be on the other side of the loading dock and be involved in actually making movies rather than just servicing them. So one day I gave a Production Manager a very competitive quote for gear and then asked for a job as a Runner on the show. A job as a Runner worked brilliantly for me as I didn't know what job on a film I wanted – I didn't really know what jobs there were – but as a Runner you get to see all departments working and interact with all of them.

Did you study?

Back in the day when I left school there were really only two options to study filmmaking. There was AFTRS and North Sydney Technical College at Gore Hill. AFTRS then was very exclusive and was skewed to more mature students rather than those straight out of school. North Sydney Tech was basically a training school for the ABC. The course was 3 years. To me, the practicality of working on a film full time and part time study was ridiculous. However, if you worked next door at the ABC the fit was perfect.

What is one piece of advice you would give to someone starting in the film industry?
Don't do what I did and think you need to know everything. I have seen many a person succeed with knowing very little, but they had ideas and drive, and knew how to surround themselves with people who did know what they didn't.

Did you think you'd be doing what you do?
Funnily enough yes.

What was your favourite job or best memory?
The Year My Voice Broke. I was a 3rd AD working in the summer of 1987 in Braidwood. It was a small six-week shoot with a great Director, brilliant script and fabulous young cast. A lot of us had worked together over the years at Kennedy Miller prior and we knew this film was a personal film for John Duigan and we were glad to be able to spend the Summer helping him make it.
And as a 1st AD, making the *Mummy 3* with Rob Cohen, a Director I really enjoy working with in Montreal and China was an amazing memory. Great fun in exotic locations.

Why would someone pursue a career as an Assistant Director?
In my case I like helping people who have great stories to tell. I don't have the skill set to write or to a lesser extent, direct, but I feel I can value add to a project by getting as much of what the Director wants on the screen and creating the space to make it happen. Warning to all – it is a very family unfriendly career to pursue.

All That

BORING PAPERWORK

8
—

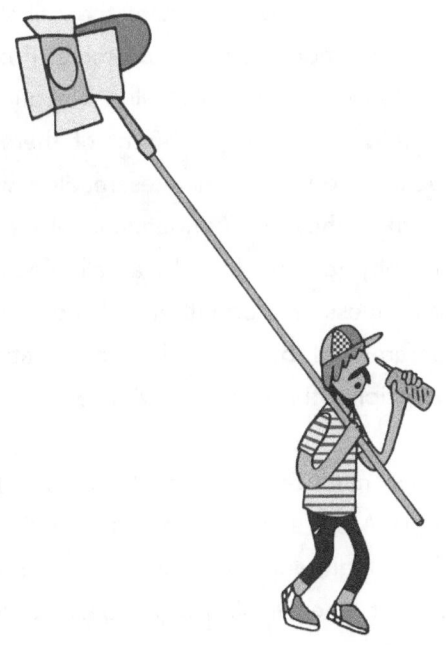

THE CALL SHEET

The call sheet is your daily bible – it is the most important piece of paper or email you can receive each day. It contains 99% of what you need to know for the day's filming, as well as info for the upcoming week and immediate contacts you may need. The call sheet is distributed by the ADs on wrap each day as a hard copy on set and an email then sent out to all crew from the production office. It is the result of much toiling by the 2nd AD and Production Coordinator, who painstakingly organise everything for the following day of filming.

I can't state enough how important the call sheet is and how much information is actually on there, if people read it closely. Often crew members will ask a question when the answer is plainly printed in front of them, only they haven't spent a couple of minutes reading what's been given to them or they don't understand where to find the information they require. Initially, a call sheet will be an overwhelming mess of information and abbreviations that's hard to comprehend, but with a little explanation, you will be able to decipher this film code with ease.

There are two main templates that are used for the call sheet. The USA/UK standard format and the Australian standard format, although many productions stick with the USA/UK format when filming in Australia. Both have the same information but are expressed differently and can take some time getting used to when you switch between the two. Often commercials will use a slightly different version as well, but the main difference is it has been bulked up containing the script, storyboards and other production details, and is often turned into a booklet as a holistic production document.

The layout of the call sheet may change slightly from job to job depending on what pieces of information they deem most appropriate and the favourite font the Production Coordinator decides to use, but all the key information will remain the same.

USA/UK TEMPLATE

Header – The header contains the title, date, shoot day number, call times, weather, above the line crew, production office details and any specific banners or messages.

MANOS ARRIBA	CALL SHEET	Date: Monday 1st June
Producer: Matthew Webb		Shoot Day: 1 of 25
Director: Andrew Seaton		
Executive Producer: Matthew Samperi		CREW CALL: 0700
Associate Producer: Nick Mutton		
Writers: Alex Ritchard/Andrew Seaton		Breakfast on arrival: 0630 - 0700
		Shooting Call: 0800
Production Office:		Sunrise / Sunset: 0651 / 1654
MINT Films		Weather: High 20 / Low 15
1/80 Wentworth Park Rd		Cloudy
Glebe NSW 2037, Office +61 2 8063 5652		

ALL PRE-CALLS MUST BE NDB / NO FORCED CALLS WITHOUT PRIOR APPROVAL FROM PRODUCER
NO UNAUTHORIZED PHOTOGRAPHY ON SET - THANK YOU

Scenes/Locations – The following block contains the scenes to be shot that day, story day, cast numbers, page count, shooting location, unit base location and closest emergency services.

SET	SCENE	CAST	D/N	PAGES	SET/ LOCATION
INT BAR ENTRANCE Brett Enters The Bar	2 pt2	1, 2, 3, 4, 7	N1	1	**INT/EXT BAR** **Kit & Kaboodle** Level 2, 33-37 Darlinghurst Rd
INT BAR NEAR DANCEFLOOR Minimal Costume, "I like it"	3	1, 2, 3, 7	N1	1	Potts Point NSW 2011
INT BAR NEAR DANCEFLOOR Brett & Flick Argue. I Was Being Minimal	4	1, 3	N1	2/8	**Unit Base & Crew Parking** Mecure Hotel 226 Victoria St
INT BAR TABLE James Arrives	5	1, 3, 4, 5	N1	1	Potts Point NSW 2011
INT BAR TABLE Brett Watches Flick	7	1, 2, 3, 4, 5	N1	1/8	**Nearest Hospital** St Vincents Hospital 390 Victoria St
INT BAR TABLE Wrong Barman	11	1, 2, 3, 4, 5	N1	2/8	Darlinghurst NSW 2010 T: +61 2 8382 1111
INT BAR DANCEFLOOR Dancing Lasoo	12	1, 2, 3	N1	2/8	
			TOTAL	3 7/8	

Equipment/Notes/Catering – Next are a few separate boxes that contain any additional equipment required for the day, special notes and instructions such as costume fittings, rehearsals or publicity interviews, and the catering breakdown for the day.

ADDITIONAL EQUIPMENT:		NOTES / SPECIAL INSTRUCTIONS		
Flex: Party Lights				
Grips: Mini Jib				
Unit: 4x Makeup Mirrors		CATERING		
Camera: Additional Red Epic Package ex. VA Hire		Crew Breakfast:	0630 - 0700	75
Props: Non-alchoholic beer/drinks		Crew Lunch:	1200 - 1245	85
Sound: Playback		A/T:	On Wrap	85

Cast/Stunts/Stand-ins/Background Artists – The cast are listed corresponding to their cast number with call times and any remarks. The stunt players may also have corresponding stunt double numbers or just a character title. Next, the stand-ins for the day are listed and all the background artists. The extras are titled under atmosphere in this instance.

#	CAST	ROLE OF	STATUS	P/U	MAKEUP/WARD		B/F	SET CALL	REMARKS
1	Ben O'Toole	BRETT	W	MOW	0715	0745	0700	0800	
2	Gus Murray	RUARAIDH	W	MOW	0715	0745	0700	0800	
3	Bella Mediarmid	FLICK	W	MOW	0630	0715	0700	0800	
4	Adam Dunn	PETE	W	MOW	0730	0745	0700	0800	
5	Alex Ritchard	JAMES	W	MOW	0900	0930	0700	0800	Called early for cast block
6	Sean Morrison	WAITER	H						
7	Renee Small	WAITRESS	W	MOW	0630	0715	0700	0800	
#	STUNT PLAYERS	ROLE OF	STATUS	P/U	MAKEUP/WARD		B/F	SET CALL	REMARKS
1A	Caleb Guinery	Brett Stunt DBL	H						

STAND-INS		IN	#	ATMOSPHERE	IN	ON SET				
BRETT	Josh Searle	0700	20	Female Partygoers	0630	0815				
RUARAIDH	Simon Edds	0700	20	Male Partygoers	0700	0815				
			1	DJ	0730	0815				

Advance Schedule – Finally, the next few days of the shoot schedule are listed under the advance schedule. This is the most accurate schedule for the coming shoot days.

ADVANCE SCHEDULE - DAY 2 - TUESDAY 2ND JUNE - INT BAR - KIT & KABOODLE				
2 pt1	N1	INT STAIRWAY Bren Enters	1	E: Nil
13A	N1	INT STAIRWAY Bandits leave	1, 8, 9, 10	E: Nil
14 pt1	N1	INT BAR At Least Be Useful	1, 2, 3, 4, 5, 6, 7, 8, 9, 10, 12	E: 41
14 pt2	N1	INT BAR Give Me Your Wallet	1, 2, 3, 4, 5, 6, 7, 8, 9, 10, 12	E: 41
15	N1	INT BAR Time To Go	1, 2, 3, 4, 5, 6, 7, 8, 9, 10, 12	E: 41
Producer: Matthew Webb				1st Assistant Director: Christopher Turner

As with all call sheets, the length and amount of information will vary depending on the size of the project. On large feature films, the call sheet may be up to five pages long containing all the information for extremely complex scenes.

AUSTRALIAN TEMPLATE

Contacts - The header includes important contacts such as emergency services, production company and the shoot day details.

Police: 02 8356 0099 (Kings Cross LAC)	Fire/Ambulance: 000	Hospital : 02 8382 1111 (St Vincents)
	MINT Films | 3/80 Wentworth Park Rd Glebe NSW 2037 | 02 8065 5652	
	Director: Andrew Seaton Producer: Matthew Webb	
	MANOS ARRIBA	
DATE: MONDAY 1ST JUNE	CALLSHEET	DAY: 1 of 30

Locations, Call Times and Banners - Below the contacts are the location addresses for the shoot including unit base, parking and shooting location and also any important banners regarding special notes for the day. Call times are located to the right with the main crew call and any pre-calls.

Producer: Matt Webb (04XX XXX XXX)

1st AD: Chris Turner (04XX XXX XXX)
2nd AD: Amy Kings (04XX XXX XXX)

Location 1: Kit & Kaboodle
Level 2, 33-37 Darlinghurst Rd
Potts Point NSW 2011

Unit Base: Mercure Conference Room
226 Victoria St
Potts Point NSW 2011

Sunrise: 0651   Sunset: 1654
Weather: Cloudy
Min: 15   Max: 20

Essentials: Loading Zone on Earl Place
Potts Point NSW 2011

Cast & Crew Parking: Mercure Hotel
226 Victoria St
Potts Point NSW 2011

HAIR/MAKEUP :   0615
COSTUME :   0615
CREW CALL (ON LOC):   0700
BREAKFAST: 0645-0715
EST WRAP: 1730

PRODUCTION NOTES:
ALL CALLS SUBJECT TO CHANGE BY THE UPM OR ADS. NO FORCED CALLS WITHOUT PRIOR APPROVAL OF LINE PRODUCER OR PRODUCTION MANAGER.
STRICTLY NO UNAUTHORISED PHOTOGRAPHY OR PERSONAL CAMERAS PERMITTED ON SET. ALL CREW MUST WEAR THEIR SECURITY PASSES. NO EXCEPTIONS

Scene Breakdown – This is what's actually being filmed on the day. The scene breakdown includes call times for cast and extras, scene length, script page count and a one-line description of the scene. This section concludes with a page count and timing of the day's anticipated shooting.

SC PART	I/E D/N	TIME PAGE	SET LOCATION	CHARACTER	ARTIST	P/U	M/UP	W/R	B/F	ON SET
				0715-0815 BUMP IN & SETUP						
				0800 Cast Block						
2 pt2	INT	1.00	BAR ENTRANCE	BRETT	Ben O'Toole	MOW	0715	0745	0700	0800
	N1	1		RUARAIDH	Gus Murray	MOW	0715	0745	0700	0800
				FLICK	Bella Modlarmid	MOW	0630	0715	0700	0800
				PETE	Adam Dunn	MOW	0730	0745	0700	0800
				WAITRESS	Renae Small	MOW	0630	0715	0700	0800
				Extras						
				20x Female Partygoers		MOW	0715	0630	0700	0815
				20x Male Partygoers		MOW	0800	0730	NA	0815
0815-0945				1x DJ		MOW	0800	0730	NA	0815
Brett Enters The Bar										
3	INT	1.00	BAR NEAR DANCEFLOOR	BRETT	Ben O'Toole					CLD
	N1	1		RUARAIDH	Gus Murray					CLD
				FLICK	Bella Modlarmid					CLD
				WAITRESS	Renae Small					CLD
				Extras						
0945-1100				As Above						CLD
Minimal Costume, "I like it"										
4	INT	0.15	BAR NEAR DANCEFLOOR	BRETT	Ben O'Toole					CLD
	N1	2/8		FLICK	Bella Modlarmid					CLD
				Extras						
1100-1200				As Above						CLD
Brett & Flick Argue. I Was Being Minimal										

Transport, Additional Contacts, Crew, Special Equipment and Notes - The remaining section will contain any peripheral information specific to that day of shooting – transport details, props, special equipment needed, additional crew members, publicity details, set visitors and various notes.

Props:	Non-alcoholic beer/drinks, DJ equipment					
Sound Playback:	Sc. 7, 12					
Special Equipment:	Additional Red Epic Package	ex. VA Hire				
	LX Package/Party Lights	ex. TRC Lighting				
	Mini Jib	ex. Damian Heckendorf				
	4x Makeup Mirrors	ex. Cato Logistics				
CATERING:						
ex Film Caterers	Breakfast	0645-0715	for	75	@ Unit Base
	Lunch:	1200-1245	for	85	@ Unit Base
	A/T:	1730-1745	for	85	@ Unit Base

Advance Schedule - As with the USA/UK template the final section of the call sheet is an advance schedule of the coming few days of shooting summarised into the one line format.

ADVANCE SCHEDULE				
SHOOT DAY: 2		TUESDAY 2ND JUNE	LOCATION: INT. BAR - KIT & KABOODLE	CC: 0700
SC	I/E	LOCATION	CAST	EXTRAS
2PT1	INT	STAIRWELL	BRETT	NIL
15A	INT	STAIRWELL	BRETT, BANDIT 1, BANDIT 2, BANDIT 3	NIL
14PT1	INT	BAR	BRETT, RUARAIDH, FLICK, PETTE, JAMES, WAITRESS, BANDIT 1, BANDIT 2. BANDIT 3, PARTY ESCAPEE	41
14PT2	INT	BAR	BRETT, RUARAIDH, FLICK, PETTE, JAMES, WAITRESS, BANDIT 1, BANDIT 2, BANDIT 3, PARTY ESCAPEE	41
15	INT	BAR	BRETT, RUARAIDH, FLICK, PETTE, JAMES, WAITRESS, BANDIT 1, BANDIT 2, BANDIT 3, PARTY ESCAPEE	41

1st Assistant Director - Christopher Turner

Maps - Maps and directions are also added to the call sheet to ensure everyone knows how to find the sometimes remote locations and also where to park and store equipment. Finding a location has become a million times easier with mapping apps on phones and in-car GPS devices. There's no need to follow pages and pages of directions anymore. However, these maps are still important for mud maps of parking and unit base layout at the location.

Other information specific to the project or day can be slotted into various sections and highlighted to attract the attention of the crew. The format of the call sheet is always similar but can be tweaked to convey the clearest message to the crew. Often crews will be lazy and only read minimal sections of the call sheet like their call time, so it's important that if anything is out of the ordinary that it is stated boldly and highlighted so no one can miss the vital stuff.

Sometimes the call time can be 'pushed' or 'pulled' by a number of minutes. This will be stamped on the call sheet with an appropriate number written in the space. E.g. 'All calls pushed by 60 minutes'. This means that everyone's call time becomes sixty minutes later than is printed on the call sheet. This can be due to a number of factors, but is usually because filming went later than expected so the call time for the next day needs to be later to avoid people breaking their turnaround. The union has placed a turnaround between finishing work and starting the next day clause in the standard contract to protect crew from the dangers associated with short breaks between shifts. This will vary in length depending on your location around the world but will be somewhere between eight to twelve hours. The reverse is also true – if filming wraps early the call can be pulled earlier. E.g. 'All calls pulled by 60 minutes'. This means that everyone's call time becomes sixty minutes earlier than what is printed on the call sheet.

Pushing the call happens much more regularly than pulling the call but make sure you read the stamp correctly when this occurs or it could be rather embarrassing when you turn up two hours late to work the next day.

HOW TO READ A SCHEDULE

There are many tricks to reading a film schedule. You'll find bundles of abbreviations, coloured strips, numbers and a million different formats – and somehow you're meant to make sense of it! Once you learn how to read the various schedules, they become second nature and entirely vital in planning your life for the next however many months. Production will issue a full shooting schedule, one liner, box schedule and day-out-of-days in pre-production. This will be amended and reissued throughout the shooting period as scenes, locations and the script change and the schedule adapts. All these schedules are produced from the breakdown the 1st Assistant Director has created with each version of the schedule useful for different departments and tasks. It's good to understand exactly how each one can be used but you will likely find yourself with a favourite (generally the box schedule as it offers the best summary of information in a simple calendar format).

FULL SHOOTING SCHEDULE
The full shooting schedule is the largest and most comprehensive version of the schedule as each subsequent version is derived from it. This schedule breaks down each scene to include as much information as possible including but not limited to: call time, sunrise and sunset

times, tides, story time of day, scene timing, location, scene heading, scene description, characters, background artist numbers, props, vehicles, costume and makeup notes, and plenty more items specific to the project. The full shooting schedule is usually only issued to HODs and those that ask for it, to save trees and avoid printing this mammoth document umpteen times.

This schedule is used in production meetings because it has all the information relevant to each department in the one document. If there is something unique to a day of shooting, it will be contained in the full schedule so that everyone is aware of that item or note. I use the full schedule in pre-production as it gives the best overview of shooting and everything that is happening, but once I've been through it a few times, I like to use the summarised version such as the one liner or box schedule to see how we are tracking throughout the shoot.

Shooting Schedule

Shoot Day # 1 Monday, May 30, 2016					
Scene # 2 PT 1	INT	Bar stairwell		Night	1/8

Brett walks up the stairs

Cast Members
1.Brett

Wardrobe
Mexican wrestling mask

Scene # 3	INT	Bar near dancefloor		Night	1

Minimal costume "I like it"

Cast Members
1.Brett
2.Ruaraidh
3.Flick
7.Waitress

Props
Beer/drinks
DJ Equipment

Set Dressing
Birthday banner
TV with photos

Background Actors
1x DJ
20x Female Partygoers
20x Male Partygoers

Camera
Slow motion package
Wardrobe
Mexican wrestling mask

Notes
Party Lighting

Scene # 4	INT	Bar near dancefloor		Night	2/8

Brett & Flick argue. I was being minimal.

Cast Members
1.Brett
3.Flick
4.Pete

Props
Beer/drinks
DJ Equipment

Set Dressing
Birthday banner
TV with photos

Background Actors
1x DJ
20x Female Partygoers
20x Male Partygoers

Wardrobe
Mexican wrestling mask

Notes
Party Lighting

Page 1

ONE LINER OR STRIPBOARD SCHEDULE

The one liner or stripboard is a summarised version of the full schedule containing each scene on – you guessed it – one line. The format highlights each day with the appropriate date and call time, location, sunrise and sunset details, then the appropriate scenes for that day. Each line contains the scene number, story day, exterior or interior location, page count, scene heading, short description of the scene, corresponding cast number of who is in the scene, number of extras and stunts in the scene, and the shoot location. Each cast member is allocated a number, which is listed in each scene. This makes it much easier to write numbers rather than longer names like Sacha Baron Cohen or Neil Patrick Harris. And you won't accidentally (and inevitably) misspell Schwarzenegger.

Sheet #: 2 1/8 pgs	Scenes: 2 PT 1	INT Night	Bar stairwell Brett walks up the stairs	1	Est. Time :10
Sheet #: 3 1 pgs	Scenes: 3	INT Night	Bar near dancefloor Minimal costume "I like it"	1, 2, 3, 7	Est. Time 1:00
Sheet #: 6 2/8 pgs	Scenes: 4	INT Night	Bar near dancefloor Brett & Flick argue. I was being minimal.	1, 3, 4	Est. Time :15
Sheet #: 7 1 pgs	Scenes: 5	INT Night	Bar table James arrives	1, 3, 4, 5	Est. Time 1:00
Sheet #: 11 1/8 pgs	Scenes: 9	INT Night	Bar dancefloor James salutes	2, 4, 5, 7	Est. Time :10
Sheet #: 12 2/8 pgs	Scenes: 10	INT Night	Bar Pete hits on a different waitress	4, 6	Est. Time :10
End of Shooting Day 1 -- Monday, May 30, 2016 -- 2 6/8 Pages -- Time Estimate: 2:45					
Sheet #: 4 1 pgs	Scenes: 2 PT 2	INT Night	Bar entrance Brett enters the bar	1, 2, 3, 4, 7	Est. Time 1:00
Sheet #: 18 3/8 pgs	Scenes: 15	INT Night	Bar Time to go	1, 2, 3, 4, 5, 6, 7, 8, 9, 10, 12	Est. Time :20
Sheet #: 16 1 pgs	Scenes: 14 PT 1	INT Night	Bar At least be useful	1, 2, 3, 4, 5, 6, 7, 8, 9, 10, 12	Est. Time 1:00
Sheet #: 17 1 pgs	Scenes: 14 PT 2	INT Night	Bar Give me your wallet	1, 2, 3, 4, 5, 6, 7, 8, 9, 10, 12	Est. Time 1:00
Sheet #: 9 1/8 pgs	Scenes: 7	INT Night	Bar table Brett watches Flick	1, 2, 3, 4, 5	Est. Time :10
End of Shooting Day 2 -- Tuesday, May 31, 2016 -- 3 4/8 Pages -- Time Estimate: 3:30					

The one liner is also colour coded to make it easier to track certain scenes at a quick glance. The colours are used to determine interior or exterior and day or night scenes. This way the scenes can be easily grouped together in the easiest order to shoot them, i.e. all interior day scenes together before exterior night scenes on the one day. The one liner is the most used schedule as it has enough information for each day giving a great overview of what is to be shot (and when), but isn't a massive wad of paper to carry around. The one liner will be issued to all crew and reissued regularly as the schedule is updated.

DESCRIPTION	STRIP COLOUR
Day Interior	White
Day Exterior	Yellow
Night Interior	Green
Night Exterior	Blue
Day Separator	Black
Week Separator	Orange
Free Day	Grey
Holiday	Red

BOX SCHEDULE

The box schedule looks like a colourful calendar and is great for a quick view of what is coming up in the shoot and where you are located. With each week given one line, each box contains the date, call time, shoot day number, scene number, location, interior or exterior, and cast, stunt and extras numbers. The aim of the box schedule is to keep information to a minimum so it's easy to read and short to print. The box schedule is extremely useful in planning the weeks ahead and when gear will need to be bumped in and out. Departments will often draw up their own version of a box schedule on whiteboards in their offices or trucks with information specific to their department added. Personally,

I keep a box schedule at the front of each of my script and schedule folders for a quick look to keep track of what is coming up, especially when night shoots are planned.

			MANOS ARRIBA Box Calendar				
wk	MONDAY	TUESDAY	WEDNESDAY	THURSDAY	FRIDAY	SATURDAY	SUNDAY
1	Day 1 cc:07:00 BAR Night Int 2 Pt1, 3, 4, 5, 9, 10 C: 5 E: 41 **Kings Cross** 1-Jun	Day 2 cc:07:00 BAR Night Int 2 Pt2, 15, 14, 7 C: 11 E: 41 **Kings Cross** 2-Jun	Day 3 cc:07:00 BAR Night Int 6, 8, 11, 12, 13 C: 5 E: 26 **Kings Cross** 3-Jun	Day 4 cc:14:00 STREET/CAR Night Ext 1, 16 C: 6 S: 1 partial night **Marrickville** 4-Jun	Day 5 cc:14:00 STREET/CAR Night Ext 17, 18, 19 C: 6 S: 1 partial night **Marrickville** 5-Jun	 6-Jun	 7-Jun

DAY OUT OF DAYS (DOOD)

The Day Out Of Days (DOOD) schedule is a breakdown of cast, extras, special equipment and vehicles for what days they are to be booked. Each category has its own schedule that is issued to those who require the information. The DOOD is formatted with the item or person down the left vertical column and the date along the top horizontal. For each day, the item or person is required an 'X' or 'W' (which stands for work) is marked in the corresponding box. This format gives a good overview of when items are spaced out over the shoot or if they are needed in consecutive days.

You will also see the letters SW (start work), FW (finish work), R (rehearsal) and H (hold), which means the item or person may be needed on that day but this hasn't been confirmed yet. Day Out Of Day schedules are used mainly by the 2nd AD and Production Coordinator to ensure cast are booked and ready for work when required. They may need to travel from overseas or interstate so their travel plans will coincide with when they are required to shoot. Other departments also use the DOOD to determine when equipment needs to be booked. As with the full schedule, the DOOD will only be issued to crew that need or ask for it as it's not useful to everyone.

Day Out of Days Report for Cast Members

	Month/Day	05/30	05/31	06/01	Co.					
	Day of Week	Mon	Tue	Wed	Travel	Work	Hold	Holiday	Start	Finish
	Shooting Day	1	2	3						
1.	Brett	SW	W	WF		3			05/30	06/01
2.	Ruaraidh	SW	W	WF		3			05/30	06/01
3.	Flick	SW	W	WF		3			05/30	06/01
4.	Pete	SW	W	WF		3			05/30	06/01
5.	James	SW	W	WF		3			05/30	06/01
6.	Waiter	SW	WF			2			05/30	05/31
7.	Waitress	SW	W	WF		3			05/30	06/01
8.	Bandit 1		SW	WF		2			05/31	06/01
9.	Bandit 2		SW	WF		2			05/31	06/01
10.	Bandit 3		SW	WF		2			05/31	06/01
11.	Bandit 4			SWF		1			06/01	06/01
12.	Party Escapee		SWF			1			05/31	05/31

MORE PAPERWORK

Forms are the worst, and there are tons you may have to fill out throughout a job. It's important you know what to fill out and how to do it correctly so other departments (particularly accounts) like you because let's be honest – they are the ones who pay you each week. You may have to fill out these forms for more senior people in your department when you are starting out, having been thrown a box full of petrol receipts and asked to claim their fuel reimbursement for months of travel. It's just one of the jobs of being a junior. Learn to do paperwork well and your department will be stoked, and so will the office and accounts. Copies of all these forms can be emailed from production or can be collected as hard copies from the production office or

ADs truck. Whenever you submit a form or receipt, make sure you photocopy it and keep a copy for yourself. Every now and again a form will be lost and it's near impossible to remember every detail you wrote down and prove the expenses without original receipts. In this case you can re-submit your photocopy and revel in the satisfaction that you don't need to spend all night refilling the forms.

TIMESHEETS

Paper timesheets are still used on the majority of jobs and need to be completed daily or weekly, and sometimes a combination of both, with the hours you have worked for each day. It's important to keep notes in a diary or phone so your hours are accurate and you have something to compare to when your pay slip comes through the following week. On most jobs, crew submit daily timesheets on wrap each day; these timesheets have the entire department's names on it for that day with the hours filled out and signed by the HOD. These are handed in to the ADs at the end of each day to allow production reports to be submitted to the studio the following day and payroll to get a head start on calculating your pay for the week.

Again, usually the most junior person in the department is responsible for completing the timesheets that are then signed by the HOD. As with the other forms, if you are doing this, a little tip is to make a photocopy of each timesheet as you will no doubt encounter crew who believe they were paid incorrectly twenty-seven days ago – hard to corroborate without the facts on paper. You can easily check your notes and they can contact accounts if any errors have been made.

LOSS AND DAMAGE REPORT (L&D)

Hopefully you only ever fill these out for an item that somebody else has broken. An L & D report is completed when a piece of equipment is lost, damaged or stolen during the cause of shooting. This ensures the item can be replaced or fixed as soon as possible and not affect filming. While filling out the L & D, add as much detail as possible with the cost of the item and where a new one can be purchased or a repair completed. This will speed up the process of getting the form approved by the UPM and the item replaced or fixed quickly.

One morning I watched a Video Split Assistant on his very first day wheel the Director's monitor across a road. The wheel hit a stick and the monitor toppled over making a horrible noise as it collided with the asphalt. He quickly pulled it back up and luckily the glass hadn't smashed but there were some dead pixels on the monitor. He had to explain the damage to his new boss on his first day of work. Sure enough, a couple of hours later, he came to me asking for an L & D form he needed to complete. He kept his job and all was fine, but do be careful when moving expensive equipment around. This is also why I never move other people's fragile equipment unless they have asked me to or given me permission.

INCIDENT REPORTS

Similar in format to the L & D form, an incident report is for any event involving people that results in injury or needs to be recorded for insurance purposes. These are mainly completed by the medic after treating someone but can also be completed by a witnessing crew member when a medic was not present. Again it is important to provide as much information as possible when completing an incident form as you may be asked to explain the situation later on to the UPM or Producer.

PETTY CASH

You may be issued with a float of cash to pay for various items throughout the shoot, especially if you are a Runner or Buyer, which can be a few hundred dollars or even a couple of thousand. These expenses can include expendables, coffees and lunches for cast and crew, or multiple other items that pop up throughout the shoot. The accounts department will have a petty cash form that is used to record the purchases with receipts and will balance your expenditure. It's important to get tax receipts when you make purchases so you can prove your expenses and balance your petty cash at the end of the job or when it runs out. Filling out the petty cash form is quite straightforward but I recommend using a calculator for all of you who failed maths at school and decided to work in the film industry because you're a true creative.

I'll say it again – make photocopies of your receipts and forms before you hand them in because you don't want to be out of pocket for an expense you can't prove without a receipt. I keep my petty cash in a separate non-transparent pencil case so it doesn't get mixed in with my personal money and I can put all my receipts in there as I make purchases.

FUEL/TOLL/MOBILE PHONE REIMBURSEMENT

If, during your deal memo, you negotiated any of these reimbursements as part of your contract, you will need to submit the appropriate forms to the accounts department to be reimbursed. There is generally a separate form for each fuel, toll and mobile phone cost. You will need to show evidence of expenditure such as monthly phone bills or fuel logs and receipts. The accounts department will appreciate you completing these forms monthly rather than handing them in as a big wad on your last day like many are guilty of doing. This also means you aren't owed a lot of money by production at the end of shooting. As I said earlier, even if you aren't filling these out for yourself, as a junior you will definitely complete these for someone else in your department. When you make a copy, simply email it to the person you have completed the form for and they will be forever appreciative.

Janty Yates
Costume Designer

2001 Academy Award Winner (Best Costume Design) –
Gladiator

Gladiator, American Gangster, Prometheus, The Martian

What was your first job in the film industry?
Assistant to the assistant to the assistant on a British Airways commercial.

Did you study?
Yes, I studied dress design, dress making and pattern cutting.

What is one piece of advice you would give to someone starting in the film industry?
You need eternal energy, never say no, and don't walk in front of the camera.

What was your favourite job or best memory?
Gladiator of course!

How does someone pursue a career in the costume department?
Have knowledge of pattern cutting and garment making, of the nature of fabrics, of the history of art, and of art finishing. Ideally be prepared to work all hours.

How did winning an Oscar change your career?

My profile was universally much higher but I owe it all to Sir Ridley Scott.

How do you approach working with high profile directors and actors?

I always approach everyone in the same way, but I try to arm myself with as much research and knowledge about the relevant project each time.

a BUNCH OF TIPS

9

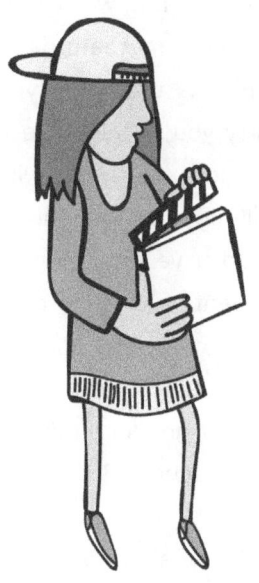

HOW TO COPE WITH THE LONG HOURS

Working in the film industry is demanding and unrelenting, commanding a high level of work ethic over extremely long hours. The lengthy hours and grueling schedule can test people's patience, strain relationships and push people to breaking point when they are stressed and pressure is applied from higher levels to achieve even more. It's important to be aware of this and protect your non-negotiables throughout a job in order to manage family life and certain significant events. You will find your outside social life will decrease dramatically for a season, as you won't have the time for mid-week dinners and you'll be sleeping the week off come Saturday. However, you will make great new friends that form your film family, and these folks will carry you through the fatigue and deliria. You will have amazing experiences, visit awesome places and do some really cool things. This all makes for great stories when you do have time to go to all the birthday parties and social events when your project concludes.

Here are some simple strategies to cope with the arduous shooting schedule and grueling industry that have helped me navigate marriage, friendships and family dynamics.

1 Get as much sleep as possible. Fatigue leads to grumpiness and exhaustion, which leads to jaded, worn out film crews; a common feature amongst overworked, experienced crew. I may not be able to stay up late binge watching Netflix and won't be able to discuss the nuances of so-and-so's social media activity the following day but at least I'll be looking after my body and mind for the long term. Sleep is incredibly important in refreshing your body after each day and the majority of people don't get enough each night.

I never book anything in early on a Saturday morning. I enjoy a nice sleep in and relaxing morning to recover from the week that's been. It allows me to enjoy my weekend being a husband and friend, or for some, to be a parent without exhibiting zombie-like features because you said 'yes' to a friend who wanted to go fishing at 6am. At times your sleep will be reduced to a bare minimum if the shooting location is a decent drive away or you are juggling young children who are interrupting your nights, but whenever you can, get as much sleep as you can.

2 Eat well and drink plenty of water. The catering will be excellent, so it will be easy to do this – but it's still important. With enough sleep, good food and plenty of water, your body should be able to function with the demands of long hours. On set catering makes it easy to eat a variety of vegetables and nutritious food that will keep your body running. I also take vitamin supplements to boost any nutrients I'm not receiving and hopefully protect me a little

from getting sick. Spending extended hours outside in all sorts of conditions will dehydrate your body unless you endeavour to guzzle plenty of water. Lots of productions provide drink bottles at the start of the job or have bottled water available on set. Recently on a job, it was so unbearably hot and humid that I was drinking 1 litre of water each hour for an entire day! Start the day by drinking at breakfast and have a bottle on your way home to replenish everything you've lost. The medic will also have hydrolytes available on those awfully hot days. If someone offers you a drink of water, just take it, even if you aren't thirsty.

3 Enjoy the break at the end of each job between contracts. Often you will have a short break between finishing one project and starting the next. It's hard to line up contracts perfectly as you will either have to leave the previous job early or the next one may not start for a few weeks. Many people stress that they are out of work for a few weeks, but considering they have worked fifty to seventy hour weeks for the last few months, hopefully there's a bit of cash with which to relax and enjoy the break. If you're not in that position, try and get a few TVCs to supplement your income while you recover. Usually for three days after I finish a job, I'm a bit of a zombie. I sleep in, read, relax and let my body recover. You'll really feel it if you do back-to-back jobs without a break. Sometimes this is necessary as you don't want to turn down the next project but

be aware towards the back end of that project that you will be prone to getting sick and exhaustion will start to affect your mood and productivity.

4 Treat your partner or spouse to something special at the end of each job. You won't have spent as much time with them over the last few months as you should have so buy them a meaningful gift, go on a holiday, hang out together – whatever it is that enriches the relationship. It's important to show that your relationship is valuable even though it may have been down the priority list with work taking so much time recently. There are too many people in the film industry who are divorced or in unhappy situations as a result of working too much, too often, or neglecting to value their spouses when they do have the time.

5 Take your +1 along to your premieres, wrap parties and any other fun social event the film crew has, whenever possible. Having the chance to meet your work friends and feel a sense of involvement in each project you do is important. When it comes to discussing the next project, they will know who you are working with again and will be supportive of your career and the opportunities it affords you as a team or family.

6 Book a holiday each year. Granted, you may not know what or where you will be working but people need holidays. Don't get caught in the trap of never booking a holiday because you might miss out on the next contract. There'll always be another job that comes around. Productions shut down over Christmas and early January so this can be a good time to have a two-week break without risking missing work. It's actually surprising how booking a holiday on random dates will often work in with the jobs you are offered anyway. My wife and I usually book a holiday at the end of a big contract – just the two of us having fun together. It doesn't have to be a really expensive, extravagant getaway, and simple is often the way to go.

After a year or two, you will become accustomed to the lengthy hours, but it will still take a week or two every time you start a job to get used to the long days again, particularly if you've had a bit of a break. At the end of a job you will find yourself exhausted and a break is often well deserved. If you do happen to do back-to-back jobs, you will definitely start to feel it toward the end of the second or third job as the exhaustion builds. By applying some of these tips, you will hopefully be more prepared to manage the exhaustive long hours and demands that a career in the film industry requires.

START WELL, FINISH STRONG

At first glance, it appears that working in the film industry provides limited job security. I struggled with this in my early career as I had dreams of buying a house and was firmly motivated to have a career that supported a future family. It was hard to reconcile how that could be possible with job contracts that typically last three to six months or commercials that last three days. It didn't help that it seemed I had to put so much effort into getting that first job, so how was I supposed to do that four or five times a year just to continue working? It's true that there is little job security in our type of contractual work, but it doesn't differ much from small business owners or tradespeople who go from job to job daily.

During my first job, I asked one of the other crew members how they make sure they get work and why aren't they worried about landing their next job. He replied calmly, 'Don't worry, the work always comes around.' And so it has. As long as you are passionate and good at what you do, don't cut corners or be lazy at work and continue to work hard for the right people, the work should continue to come in and you'll find yourself doing some jobs you'd only dreamt of. You will inevitably have some down time between jobs, but this is generally an opportunity to recover from working such longs hours, spend some time with your family or a chance to focus on some personal projects you may be developing.

Starting a new contract every three to four months does have its positives and negatives. If you are not enjoying one particular job, you can see light at the end of the tunnel.

On the other hand, you have to frequently experience that strange feeling of starting high school every few months. You have to get to know a whole new group of crew and discover how you fit in with the unique dynamics on each project. Starting strong in that first week is crucial in establishing yourself. This by no means requires aggressive or assertive dominance but rather, doing an excellent job from day one. This will become easier as you discover what preparation is best in pre-production.

Make sure you spend time before the job reading your script, learning cast and crew names, familiarising yourself with any new equipment and forgetting any bad attitudes or grudges from previous jobs. Giving that extra little bit in the first few weeks can really set you up amongst your superiors as a hard-working, valuable crew member.

You need to make sure you are fulfilling your tasks so your new bosses are pleased, but take care not to fall into the trap of doing other people's jobs if they aren't. Whatever you find yourself doing in that first week, you'll have to continue doing until the end of the shoot even if it's not part of your role. Make sure you know who's in what department; it's always embarrassing when you ask a standby props person to move 'their' sound trolley. Spend time at lunch sitting with other departments so you get to know them a bit more – it will then be much easier to ask for their help when you need a lamp moved or a trolley carried upstairs. After a few years, you'll find you already know a large majority of the crew and it becomes easier and easier to start jobs each time.

You are bound to make some mistakes throughout your career. Hopefully not career-ending mistakes but I guarantee some of them will be hilarious when you look back on them. At the time it will feel like the world is about to end, you will never get hired again and you are terrible at your job. The world isn't about to end, you will get hired again and you are continually learning and improving at your job.

One of the best things to combat a mistake is to own it. Admit to it, fix it and don't do it again. When a PA makes a mistake but owns up to it to me, all I am left to do is help them resolve the issue, teach them what they should have done and they have earned some of my respect for confessing to the problem. Some people try to blame others, hide the mistake or deny any knowledge. Eventually this will come back to haunt them as they won't learn from these mistakes and move on in their career.

I've made plenty of mistakes in my jobs. From simple things like wrong coffee orders to embarrassing days of calling cut when you think the Director has said it but really they just mumbled something to themselves. There is a saying that you are allowed to make mistakes on a film set just as long as you don't make the same mistake twice. If you continually forget the wrong coffee, how can they trust you to cue a set of stunt people where their safety relies on timing and your cue? Even if it's hard, and you are worried about the ramifications, own your mistakes, learn from them and move on.

You will inevitably have hard days and hard jobs. They can be physically demanding, longer hours than usual, jobs on location, jobs while you deal with personal situations or the crew just doesn't seem to gel together. Often I learn the most from my hardest days. I learn about my capacity and what I can handle as well as little things to get me through a tougher job, whether it is simple skills or coping mechanisms.

My very first job remains as one of the hardest jobs for me. A TV drama that involved many remote locations in a position I handled but was completely new to. Crew would go out of their way to see what I could cope with as the new guy. Not like they were bullying me, but more as a test to see if I had what it took to stick it out in this industry. Luckily, I had some great people in my department who trained me well and supported me through the job. I finished the job having pushed my body to something I'd never done before working sixty-hour weeks and now could complete the role of a 3rd AD. I still had more to learn and it wasn't for another two years before I became completely comfortable in my skills for that position. Even now I still look back to what I learnt on those hard days on my first ever TV job.

The saying 'you're only as good as your last day' is pretty spot on in the film industry. It's important that you finish jobs well as it is the final memory for a HOD looking to offer work to you in the future, or the impression you need to have crew members speak favourably when your name gets discussed for potential jobs in months to come. By the end of jobs, people are sleep deprived, short tempered and will not give you the grace you had at the start of the job. In the last few months, you should have learned new skills and progressed to take a bit of workload from your superiors. Put in that little bit extra in the last week to help everybody get through.

You will also find there are opportunities towards the end of a shoot to take a bit more responsibility and prove your skills. This may come due to other crew members moving onto other projects or a 2nd unit or splinter unit being established to get extra shooting done before the shoot wraps up. Be ready to step up and embrace the opportunity, as it will show that you are ready to move up to that next position when the time is right.

A week or two before the end of shooting, people will start discussing what the next job is. It'll be the hot goss at breakfast, lunch and in between takes. It's like a scouting program as people try and figure out what contract they should be chasing next or surveying which crew they will be working with on the next job. The good thing about this is you may hear about exciting jobs and can gain crucial insight so you know who to contact for available positions. Once a job starts pre-production, crewing it is all over pretty quickly with departments being sorted around people who know each other. There is a small scramble to get the best crew that are available for those dates and build a department that will work well together. If you do hear about a job you'd like to get on to, pick up the phone as soon as possible and find out if you can send a CV over to your prospective employer. Even if you miss out to start with, they will have your name in the back of their mind for any additional roles or casual days, or if someone cancels at the last minute.

Here's some simple tips for ensuring you get that next contract:

1 Coffee Skills
Learn to make good coffee! It's a simple thing that goes a long way. Everybody loves a great personal barista.

2 Early Bird
Get to work early. Be the first person there to open the truck or make the coffees. If you are taking pressure off your superiors, they will certainly consider you for the next job.

3 Ego Check
Don't think you know everything and always be open to taking advice.

4 Open Ears
Listen to everything. Even conversations at lunch can be invaluable opportunities to hear what shot is next or that the schedule for next week might be changing.

5 BS Radar
Don't believe everything you hear on-set. There are many rumours that will go around set. 'Next week is all night shoots'. 'We are working this Saturday'. Be careful what you believe and more importantly who you hear it from. Some people are, frankly, idiots.

6 Own Your Mistakes
You will make mistakes along the way, especially when starting out. Admit to them, fix the problem, move on and don't make it again.

7 Radio Star
Learn to use your radio properly. There's nothing worse than someone who uses a radio the way my grandmother uses an iPad.

8 **Open Your Eyes**
Before you ask a question, check the answer isn't on the call sheet already. 90 per cent of the time, it will be there, so use your eyes, brain and initiative.

9 **Mr Smiley**
Have a good attitude. Even if you made a huge mistake yesterday, today is a new day to prove why they hired you.

10 **Relationships Build Careers**
Your CV may be awesome but at the end of the day people hire crew they know or are given recommendation. It's important to maintain good relationships throughout the broad film industry, as you never know where your next job can come from.

NIGHT SHOOTS

Night shoots suck. Everybody will tell you that. Nobody wants to be racing home trying to beat the sun coming up, and as your head hits the pillow the rest of the family wakes you up, or even worse, the neighbours are renovating their bathroom this week, or the council is doing road works just outside your window.

Unfortunately, night shoots are a part of almost every project. To capture exterior scenes in the dark, there's really no other way than shooting these scenes at night.

Sometimes DOPs experiment with day for night (D4N) shoots and convert the sunlight into a nighttime look in post or with filters on the camera, but for the majority, it's all about the sun going down and shooting in the dark. Typically, you will start around 5pm and go until about 5am, or whenever the sun sets and rises for that time of year. It often becomes a frantic rush to capture the last shot as the sun is starting to pop on the horizon, threatening to ruin your scene but as soon as that sun comes up, you know it's time to pack up your equipment and head home. It can be hard to juggle a family while on night shoots as you have only had a couple of hours of sleep when they are waking up for their day, but I do know some crew who enjoy this as it's a chance for them to take their children to school or daycare. They can then return to bed and get a few more hours sleep before heading off to work in the mid-afternoon. After a few night shoots, you will find what works best for you and discover ways you can sleep anywhere and at any time throughout the day.

Sometimes the schedule will have half-day-half-night shoots, which involve shooting a few daytime scenes from midday until the sun goes down and then shooting a few night scenes before wrapping at around midnight. This also allows the DOP to capture magic hour, which can be beautiful lighting for certain exterior scenes. Personally, I enjoy half-day-half-night shoots as it allows me to go for a surf or tick off a few personal errands before heading to work. It means you do miss dinner with the family and again don't get time to watch *The Bachelor* but it's way better than a full night shoot and having to sleep in the day. Unfortunately, night shoots are a part of most shooting schedules so you need to find a way to deal with working all night and sleeping in the day.

WE ARE ALL ON THE SAME TEAM

As the shoot gets drawn out and the crew becomes tired and more irritable, it is important to remember you are all on the same team working for the same common goal. Even though the crew is broken down into smaller departments, they still make a large team that is employed to create the film together. They are there to bring to life the ideas of the Director and Producer in the most creative and efficient ways. This can be difficult when the Director is hard to work for or when personalities clash over weeks of working closely together. Everybody is different and will find working with certain personalities easy or difficult. It is always best practice to give people the benefit of the doubt in most circumstances and get on with your job even if they are causing issues.

On some jobs, I find certain crew members will really grind me but when I work with them on the next job, we get along really well. This can be because I am run down and easily irritated at the time or they may be dealing with a difficult boss or issues in their own personal life that was causing them to act out of character. At the end of the day, just remember you aren't saving lives and you are all on the same team. It's easy to react badly when someone yells at you or is rude for no reason but it's best to let things go and continue doing your job. Obviously you'll get the most out of your career in film land if you respect others, react graciously to all on set and actively have as much fun as you possibly can.

BUYING EQUIPMENT AND WORKWEAR

No matter which department you find yourself in, you will be required to buy some specific equipment and workwear to help you survive your working environment. This expectation could range from a variety of tools for grips and electrics, a standby kit containing all kinds of interesting items for the art department, a makeup kit for makeup artists and of course wet weather clothing for everyone in the crew. Everybody has his or her own preferred tools, so it is up to you as to what you eventually purchase. Have a look at what other people use and decide how to build your ultimate kit over your first few jobs. You don't need to purchase it all at once, spending your entire first paycheck, but can acquire your tools over the first few years as you decide what you prefer and discover the path you will take. Buying quality brands is recommended, as even though they may cost a little bit more up front, you'll be using these tools every day to earn your income. See it as a small investment in your future as a filmmaker, and remember, some of the items you purchase can be claimed as a tax deduction so hold onto your receipts.

You will find yourself spending long amounts of time in the outdoors dealing with the sun, rain, extreme heat or even snow. Outerwear will be specific to the conditions you expect to encounter in your climate but as a minimum, I would consider buying a top quality long rain jacket, wet weather pants, waterproof hiking boots, down jacket or vest, light gloves and a beanie. This may seem obvious to some but I have seen many crew members spend hours in the rain, mud or blazing sun without the appropriate outerwear. This only makes an already difficult job even more unrelenting. I have a bag that I leave in my car all year round with all my jackets and gear in it. You'd be surprised how many times my down jacket has come out in the middle of summer or when I use my rain jacket on a perfect sunny day as we have rain effects and I find myself standing under it for a few hours. You can never be too prepared for the conditions you'll find yourself in at work.

SHOULD I GET A CREWING AGENT?

You will discover there are a variety of crew agents that represent many workers in the film industry. Crew agencies do not work like acting agents, but work as receptionists and diary keepers, being the first point of contact for productions who will call to book you for jobs and dates.

They are generally specific to each city or state and have crew for every position you could think of in a production. Although an agent may not search out work for you as an acting agent does, many productions (particularly for TVCs) use these agents to book crew on jobs. They also send out newsletters keeping you informed about upcoming productions and potential HODs you can contact to apply for jobs. There are definitely reasons for getting an agent but for some it might feel like a waste of cash. I believe it never hurts to have your name read out in front of producers, production managers and HODs as often as possible as they scour for crew, but if you are on long form drama, you will be paying fees for months when you're already completely booked out. It can be a good place to start when you are entering the industry as they will try to get you work, however it will generally be short form jobs so if you only want to work on features or TV series it may not pay dividends.

I have kept my membership for five years now even though I have maintained consistent full time work on long form dramas. At a cost of roughly $1000/year after the tax return, it's not a huge spend. Occasionally I will pick up a TVC in my time between contracts through the agency but often it is with someone I've worked with before or a recommendation by someone I know and they have just gone through my agent for ease of booking. Some would argue that it's a waste of money for me, but I do find the monthly newsletters helpful in trying to plan upcoming jobs.

Crewing agents are much more prevalent in Australia and the UK with only a few scattered around the USA. They are all slightly different in each location but are a good place to start your research for potential contacts and job opportunities. Apart from deciding whether you want to join an agency or not, these crewing agent websites are also good places to start building your list of contacts to send your CV to when you are applying for jobs or work experience. You can view different department roles and even people's CVs and contact details that can be extremely useful.

The main crewing agents in Australia are:
- Auscrew (www.auscrew.com.au)
- Top Technicians (www.toptechsmanagement.com.au)
- Freelancers (www.freelancers.com.au)
- Calling All Crew (www.callingallcrew.com)
- CrewTube (www.crewtube.com.au)
- Essential Crew (www.essentialcrew.com.au)

Membership ranges from \$40 to \$140 a month, which is tax deductible. There is also a phone App called CrewUp that is much cheaper and offers a similar service through their online application where you create a profile and production companies can book you through your calendar.

The main crewing agents in the USA are:
- All Crew Agency (www.allcrewagency.com)
- The Crew Store (www.thecrewstore.com)
- Crews Control (www.crewscontrol.com)

The main crewing agents in the UK are:

- My Crew (www.my-crew.co.uk)
- Gems Agency (www.gemsagency.co.uk)
- We Crew For You (www.wecrew4u.com)

It's completely up to you whether you want to pay for this type of service and each individual situation will be different depending on your career aspirations and contacts you already have.

THE UNIONS

Unions are prevalent in most industries and countries around the world and the film industry is no different. For the fee the member pays, the union represents the working conditions of the employee to their employer and does any negotiations needed regarding minimum wages, working conditions, workplace safety, government lobbying and hiring and firing procedures. The union regularly visits the crew on set to monitor working conditions and discuss upcoming projects and news. Sometimes a vote is taken to address key issues with all members present allowed to vote. The fees for the union are usually based on how much an individual earns, but differ depending on which union it is. To join most unions, you simply fill out a form and pay your fees to apply, while some have stringent requirements an individual must meet such as working a set number of days as a trainee before being granted full membership. This allows the unions to represent the highest class of workers and possess strong power when negotiating deals with the studios.

I would urge all crew starting out to join the union once they have established themselves and have committed to the film industry as a career. At times you may feel that the union doesn't do much and you are paying fees for nothing but they do a lot of work you don't necessarily see. The more people who join up, the more staff they can put on, which equals better results for members. At the end of the day, I pay $13 a week to the MEAA, which is not going to break my budget but helps the crew in Australia have a unified voice as a global film industry.

AUSTRALIAN UNIONS

The Media Entertainment and Arts Alliance (MEAA) is the main union for film and TV crew members in Australia. There's also Screen Producers Australia (SPA) for producers and The Australian Director's Guild (ADG) for directors. The MEAA's main functions are to protect the rights of all Australian film and TV crew members in negotiations with production companies and producers, and to lobby the government about legislation and funding. You don't need to be affiliated with any unions in the Australian film industry to get jobs and it is completely up to the individual should they wish to join.

USA UNIONS

The film industry in the USA is heavily unionised and many jobs require a worker to be affiliated with a union or association to be allowed to work in this capacity. These unions can be broken down into above-the-line unions (creative individuals – producers, directors, designers, actors) and below-the-line unions (individuals who perform the physical production of the film). Above-the-line unions include: Producers Guild of America (PGA), Directors Guild of America (DGA), Writers Guild of America (WGA), Alliance of Motion Picture and Television Producers (AMPTP) and Screen Actors Guild & American Federation of Television and Radio Artists (SAG-AFTRA). Below-the-line unions include: I.A.T.S.E, Teamsters Union, Motion Picture Editors Guild (MPEG), Animation Guild, Location Managers Guild International (LMGI), and Motion Picture Sound Editors.

When you have decided what line of work you would like to pursue in your career, it's important to do some research so you can determine what union you should join and how to go about joining it. It can be a laborious process of many years of training and low pay before being granted membership and enjoying the vast benefits of union membership.

UK UNIONS

The union situation in the UK is balanced somewhere between the USA and Australia, having good membership numbers representing a large portion of the workers but the industry is not considered to be unionised. The

Broadcasting, Entertainment, Cinematograph and Theatre Union (BECTU) is the union for workers in film, broadcasting and the arts in the UK, while Equity represents actors, performers, choreographers, stunt personnel and other individuals working in the entertainment industry. You don't have to be affiliated with these unions to work in the UK but you may benefit from membership if this is your career.

Kyle Gardiner
Stunt Performer/Coordinator

Pirates of the Caribbean: Dead Men Tell No Tales, Alien: Covenant, The Wolverine, Hacksaw Ridge

What was your first job in the film industry?
I was hired as a stunt performer for a scene in a well-known Australian TV show *Stingers*.

Did you study?
I studied, but for a completely different field of work! I completed a Bachelor of Commerce. In regards to studying for stunts, I guess I unknowingly had been studying my whole life. I grew up training as a gymnast, a springboard and tower diver and also participated in a number of other sports throughout my youth. I then eventually discovered the world of live show performance and continued my skill/performance development there.

What is one piece of advice you would give to someone starting in the film industry?
Talent. I was always told you can't fake talent, so just be good at what you do! Some people are naturally talented, others have to work at it. Do what you have to do to be talented and make that your focus.

Did you think you'd be doing what you do?
Not for a second! I had always wanted to be a physiotherapist growing up. Somehow I got sidetracked into finance, but my love for performing, competing and testing myself always stayed with me and eventually took over.

What would you be doing if you didn't work in the film industry?
I would most likely still be a stockbroker/financial advisor.

What was your favourite job or best memory?
Fool's Gold. I spent months swimming, scuba diving and driving boats and getting paid for it. My wardrobe consisted of boardshorts and a t-shirt and that was the job that led to my first Taurus World Stunt Award nomination.

What's so great about the stunts department?
Every day and every job is different! It is creative and challenging both physically and mentally. Sometimes it feels like we are playing Cowboys and Indians like we did as children and making a living from it!

Why would someone pursue a career as a stunt performer or stunt coordinator?
Usually it is a passion for performing mixed with a love of film. It always starts with performing first and then some will decide to make the transition to coordinating. Most stunt performers come from an elite background in a particular field of sport and when their competitive career ends it is a way to put all those years of training and discipline to use.

How do you approach working with high profile directors or actors?
Every actor and director is different and should be approached as such. I always use meetings to gauge their expectations and style and try to implement that into my work method. Understanding their expectations, needs, wishes and vision is the best way to deliver the best product possible.

Film
LIFE

10
—

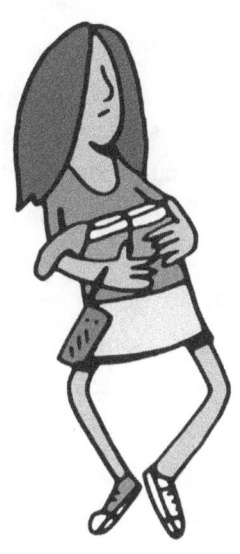

THE FOUR THINGS YOU'LL GET FROM EACH JOB

When considering a job or contract offer, there are four things that I assess in the decision process. Everyone will be working for one or more of the following on each job depending on their experience and situation: money, a film credit, experience and connections.

MO' MONEY MO' PROBLEMS

Often work is work and you do it because you have to pay bills and live. Most people live like this and getting paid is definitely one of the biggest drivers, let's be honest. I negotiate a rate that I am satisfied with on each contract and the production honours the agreement by paying me after each week of work. On some jobs you may not get offered as much money as you were expecting, or you may intentionally take a pay cut to do a certain job because you believe in it and they genuinely don't have the budget to pay your usual rates. Sometimes I do work for less money and this is generally to get a higher credit, gain more experience or work with someone I admire or are good friends with. Money is a big factor when considering a role because you need it to live and feel rewarded for your hard work but the film industry is a creative one so there are other factors that come into it when deciding upon a project.

TAKE THE CREDIT

When moving up a level in your position you may not get offered the same deal as an experienced crew member in that role but over time you can negotiate higher rates as your experience increases in these roles. In this situation, you aren't purely doing the job for money but for a higher credit. It may be a smaller project where you get offered the next position up to test your skills or someone you've worked with for many jobs may give you an opportunity to move up once they deem you are ready. Moving into a new position is always a bit harder as you are out of your depth and really have to concentrate on your job every day to make sure you are covering all your new responsibilities.

Occasionally you may say yes to a project purely because you want the credit on your CV as you know it will work in your favour in the long term. The money may be less than you want but having this particular credit will be of an advantage later in your career. It may be with an iconic Director, a studio you are trying to impress or a type of project you are trying to pursue.

EXPERIENCE

Every job will be an experience – some are good, and some you'd rather forget. Early on in your career, you may even consider doing some work for free just to get the experience. Even now I sometimes do a small job for free if it's for a good group of people or charity. This may be a music video, short film or content for a not-for-profit organisation. I say yes to these jobs because the experience is enjoyable with good people and often it allows me to practice my skills of producing without a huge amount of pressure. There are also the fun experiences you can have while shooting. This can be saying yes to a job because it's being shot overseas or interstate or simply just working with some close friends for a period.

CONNECTIONS

Who you know doesn't just apply to getting your first job but also securing future jobs, so often when considering a role, the connections I will make from that job can also be the big draw card. I've worked jobs with directors and producers I admire, large studios that will continue to give me work and also fun people I just like seeing each day. The role might be one I've done many times before so I'm not exactly upskilling and the credit might not be great for the CV but working with these certain people makes the job worth it.

When negotiating and contemplating what jobs to take, I always consider these four factors and make sure the role is fulfilling at least one of them. Sometimes I even find myself thinking I said yes to a job because of a certain connection that turns out to be a dead-end but then I'm offered a higher position towards the end of the shoot when someone leaves and everything changes. I try not to blindly chase money as that's not the greatest motivator to maintain commitment for the long hours and grueling work, which is a staple of this career. It's a privilege to make films with top people around the world so I never want it to feel like I'm only doing this to pay my mortgage. I can assure you there are much easier jobs to do if you only want to pay off the bills.

THE CIRCLE OF FILM LIFE

Work, drink, sleep, repeat. This is what some people believe the film life consists of. Early starts, beers on wrap, minimal sleep and the same the following day. This can be accurate, but many people do manage to balance some kind of social and family life with a film career. Although every job has its own feel and challenges, they all seem to follow a pretty simple formula for each stage of production.

It begins with pre-production where you spend a few weeks reading, researching and preparing for the shoot, and also catching up with old friends you haven't seen in awhile. You can afford to have longer lunches and visit departments on the lot to see how everyone is. There's a great sense of teamwork as the freshly formed crew discovers where this project is heading and predicts what the dynamics on set will be like. Usually everyone is looking and feeling fresh after some good sleep and relaxation in between the previous jobs. Pre-production is a fairly relaxing time with ten-hour work days up until the final week where you have to cram in everything you haven't finished to be ready for shoot day one.

The first shoot day arrives and even though most people feel under prepared and wished they had one more week to finish off all the prep they didn't get around to, production goes headfirst into the shoot. The first week can be a hard slog as everyone finds how he or she fits into the process, particularly if the crew hasn't worked much together before. Relationships formed in pre-production will be tested as everyone pushes to bring their best to the table but inevitably, compromises are a part of the filmmaking process. Week one holds an air of excitement and joy as something that had merely been words on a page and sketches on a storyboard takes shape and now comes to life for the Director.

Usually by week two your body is feeling the grind from week one and you start to remember the long weeks you have ahead of you. I still haven't decided if filmmakers have the memory of a goldfish because after a really hard job, we seem to forget it immediately and sign up for the next one. Of course, it is possible that we actually have the greatest job in the world, as we get to create something new every day and find ourselves in locations you would have never visited with your 'second' family.

I've coined the term the 'three week grumps' because every crew I have worked with suffers this. It can be the third week of filming or even three weeks after a hiatus or extended break that people suffer this condition. It seems to be when the crew reaches a threshold of lack of sleep but their bodies haven't quite adjusted to the long hours and litres of coffees ingested hourly. Young crew members beware: week three is when people will be snappy, angry and have fire in their eyes. Keep your head down and do your job as best you can to make it through this period. I guarantee you'll notice it yourself having less patience and being easily irritated.

From week four until about week eight the crew finds their stride and can be very productive. Everyone knows each other enough now to trust them to do their job and people relax a little bit as they don't need to impress anyone anymore. Production ticks along as you cross out each day on the box schedule. You'll form new friends and hopefully improve at your role as you continue to do it every day. On smaller jobs, the crew will find satisfaction on seeing the end of the job approaching in the eighth or ninth week as this can be the entire shoot, but on larger jobs, the shoot can last up to twenty-five weeks so you are only just getting started.

From about ten weeks into the shoot the crew will start a slow descent into exhaustion. Working sixty to seventy-hour weeks on your feet slowly takes a physical toll and even though you start with the best attitude, and are polite and courteous at the beginning, you will soon find your patience tested and will drop the niceties in most situations. It happens to the best of them. That is why it's so important to make sure you catch up on sleep on the weekend and do whatever you can to stay healthy.

As you near the end of a shoot, the days and weeks finish quicker and before you know it the last shoot day is upon you. Presents are handed out, wrap parties are organised and everyone thanks everyone for the hard work they've put in. It seems that after every job the common phrase is 'That was a tough one, but I enjoyed it'. People plan their next jobs and discuss who they'll be working with again. There is a sense of satisfaction for completing the project and an air of excitement for the new projects people are discussing.

At the conclusion of the shoot, you may have a small amount of post-production time to clean and organise equipment. This is similar to pre-production with a relaxed environment and shorter working days. Everybody feels a sense of accomplishment and hopefully some pride in what they've made together. It'll be a while before you get to see the finished product but you'll get to see everyone again at the cast and crew screening in a year or so.

Even though it appears making a film can be a sprint to get it made in a certain amount of time with a limited budget, the overall project is a marathon where you need to manage fatigue and exhaustion to finish in one piece. I've heard it said that the best two days on a film are the day you get offered the job and the wrap day. You feel so excited when the phone call comes in and you have been hired for a big film or promoted to the next position. You then slog it out for six months and can't wait to finish the job only to take a phone call to do it all over again. We're a psychotic bunch.

CASUAL DAYS/ADDITIONAL DAYS

When you are not contracted for an extended period of time on a TV drama or feature, it's a good idea to balance your down time with some casual days on various productions. Often referred to as additional crew, you will be assisting with larger shoot days where bigger scenes involve more equipment, cast and extras or various elements that are specific to that day. The crew numbers are increased on these scheduled days to cope with the demand for bigger scenes. For these days you will negotiate a day rate with the UPM, which should be fairly consistent with market rates and is approximately 30-50 per cent higher than your usual day rate. These days will be arranged by your booking agent should you have one or you may be contacted directly by a HOD or UPM you have worked with in the past.

Most of the time these days will come as a result of having worked with someone in the crew that are full time on the shoot, or someone may have recommended you. The casual days are a great way to earn some income without the usual responsibility of being a core crew member. It's also a good opportunity to expand your network and meet a bunch of new film people or simply just stay in touch with people you already know. I personally love to work as an Additional Assistant Director when I'm not on a full time contract as it's a good day rate and you don't have the usual responsibility of a full time role. One tip is to know how much a day rate is for your position. Many sneaky UPMs will try and squeeze the rate as low as possible but if you know the market rates you can negotiate confidently knowing you are correct.

FREELANCE WORK

At some stage in your career you may choose to be a full time freelancer, or else dabble here and there in between contracts. The benefits of freelancing are numerous: you can wear shoes far less, work your own hours depending on the project, charge higher rates than you'd be able on a full time gig and choose the work you do so that you have higher creative control, which suits all those insufferable control freaks out there (you know who you are).

Some people decide to freelance when they have young children as it allows them to work the hours they want to and earn a higher amount for fewer hours, although freelancing can be a challenge at times if you have a quiet period and go for a few weeks without work. It's important you continually contact your network of employers and discuss upcoming work or projects to minimise any downtime. Some people love freelancing as it gives them a more relaxed and open lifestyle, but others can't handle the inconsistencies of work and find the pressure of this financial burden too heavy. Good clients will pay your invoice on time but occasionally frustrating clients will struggle to even return an email when you have sent them an invoice weeks prior and still have not been paid. A good tip is to talk to other freelancers about their experiences and see whether you think this would be right for you or not.

Freelancing in Australia involves invoicing through your Australian Business Number (ABN) for the work you have completed. You will pay taxes through your ABN rather than as a Pay As You Go (PAYG) employee and will have to submit a tax return as a business through a registered accountant at the end of the financial year. It's easy to get an ABN. You can do it online and it's free. I would recommend this for young people starting out to set up their business and discuss the running of this with an accountant. This will allow you to say 'yes' to any work requiring an ABN. It's the easiest way for someone to employ you in the short term, as they don't need to deal with your tax or superannuation. They pay your invoice and that simply goes down as an expense in their book keeping.

As a freelancer, you won't have any sick pay, holiday pay or superannuation paid by your employer so it's important to put some aside from each job to cover these circumstances. Young people like myself sometimes neglect to consider the future and can overlook the cumbersome world of superannuation, but if you don't do anything about this for ten years of freelancing, it can really affect your lifestyle when you choose to retire.

One thing you will also need to consider is your insurances if you are freelancing. There is public liability insurance, professional indemnity insurance and also workers compensation. I'm not an expert on these so you would be best speaking with an insurance broker, or the MEAA who offer some of these services.

Personally, I freelance on TVCs and other branded content between my longer form contracts. I have an ABN that I invoice from for this work and am able to claim certain expenses throughout the year as a result. Whenever I freelance, my rates are substantially higher, as I need to consider the factors of running my own business and that the work is more sporadic. I can earn the same from doing three days of freelancing as I can from five days of full time work, but the work is irregular and I prefer the security of longer form projects and the gratification of the work involved.

When you are starting out and trying to set yourself up, you can say yes to any jobs and opportunities with an ABN so I'd suggest you do the simple online form and set yourself up from the start. It does make your tax return slightly more complex at the end of the financial year but it's absolutely worth the effort to be able to earn extra income between longer form projects.

IT'S A WRAP (PARTY)

The wrap party is a celebratory gift from the Producer or Production Company to the cast and crew on completion of shooting. These parties can be extremely lavish and lots of fun with great venues, open bar tabs and often a short preview screening of some of the scenes from the film. This is usually the first chance the crew gets to let their hair down after a crazy shooting schedule and sometimes things can get out of hand. The crew are generally tired and run down and keen to drink – a lot.

For those going to their first wrap party it may seem like the golden ticket to drinking as much as you possibly can at the open bar, having only been paid minimal rates for your first job. Just make sure you are aware of whom you are partying with. These aren't your schoolmates anymore where anything goes and you share stories of how stupid that weekend was on Monday at lunch. These are your employers for the next job. Some of your department may have your back but you don't really want a UPM holding your hair back while you vomit in the toilets. Or maybe you do and think it's a funny story to regale at a later point, who knows?

Wrap parties are a great opportunity to spend a fun night reminiscing over funny stories from the shoot and building better relationships with those that will hopefully continue to employ you. My advice is have a great time but be mindful of whose company you are in, and that there could be possible ramifications for accidentally punching the DOP in the face while cutting sick on the dance floor. You can go wild the following weekend without your career on the line.

Another insight is that most of the crew relax a lot more at wrap parties, so it's a good time to speak with that senior crew member that you have all the respect in the world for but haven't had the opportunity on set to approach. After a few drinks they are generally a lot easier to chat to and you may learn a thing or two while they recount stories and offer advice.

Wrap parties are a well-deserved celebration and are enjoyed by all in the film industry but at least until your career is firmly established, make sure you make wise decisions around the people who can make or break your career.

WHAT TO DO NOW

Beg, bribe, harass and offer to work for free. Your main goal now should be to find a job that is at least remotely pointing you in the direction you want your career to develop. Don't take no for an answer and don't give up if the first few opportunities turn out to be dead ends. As I said earlier, use websites such as crewing agents to email HODs and production companies your CV to see if you can get lucky initially. If you have any distant connections to someone who works in film or TV, make every effort to contact them and see if they can help you with your first job. I have found that everybody was at some stage in their career helped by someone else, so most people are happy to help where they can.

I always make an effort to offer advice or pass on CVs when someone young contacts me and makes the effort. The responsibility is on you to contact them and chase them though. Don't expect a call back if all you do is leave a voice message. If they don't respond to your first email after a week, send them another one or give them a quick call. They may have missed it and I can guarantee it will be at the bottom of their priorities, so they may need a little reminder. If nothing comes up after a few months, and it may take a few months or even longer to have a breakthrough, you can offer to work for free for two weeks to prove your skills or try and get work placement on their next project either full time or part time balanced with another source of income. Once you've been given this first opportunity, work hard, build your network and discover where you want to head in your career on set.

It's a great habit to build a list of contacts you will email when unemployed to see if they have any projects coming up you can work on. At least for the first few years it's important to get your name out there and work with different people. Send these emails to individuals; never write a bulk email to everyone on your list. Usually in the last week or two of a shoot, if I haven't negotiated my next job, I will send out a few emails to people I know who have projects coming up letting them know I'm available soon. I attach a recent CV and if needed, offer to drop into their offices or catch up over a drink.

Redo your CV! I'm still yet to receive a CV from someone starting out that is appealing. We receive hundreds of CVs for each job and almost every single one is a drab Microsoft Word layout using Times New Roman to tell the world how fabulous and deserving of this job they are. Next. There's no point even reading the information because I'm already bored by the look of it. You don't need to try and oversell your past work and experiences. The truth is you don't have any, but that's okay. You are trying to get your first job. The best thing you can do is stand out from the pile of bland, black and white CVs. Add some colour, use a new layout, and keep it simple and fresh. There are plenty of cheap and easy to use CV templates available on the Internet you can adjust for yourself or pay a graphic designer friend to make something that really sticks out. It might cost you a few dollars or some beers, but it could mean the difference between starting your dream career or your CV getting tossed aside with all the other drivel. The film industry is a creative one, so most people that work in it appreciate a good aesthetic. Get your CV looking sleek and hopefully someone will take a risk on you and give you a job.

It's also great to keep developing your own personal projects, particularly if you want to direct, write or produce. This will continue to sharpen your skills and help create a showreel that will become valuable in the years to come. Team up with other like-minded people, an aspiring DOP, or a cool new Production Designer that can help bring your projects to the next level as well as giving them a platform to express their skills. It's win-win for everybody. These projects don't have to have large budgets. Work with the resources you have. You never know what connections you will make from collaborating on a project. I've recommended people for jobs that I met through unpaid short films so keep up the side projects!

The truth: jobs in the film industry are competitive. It's a fun, crazy and challenging career that allows you to express your creativity every day, meet interesting people, go to beautiful locations and earn good money while doing it. It's not an easy career and it can be draining constantly chasing new contracts every few months, but after a few years you will cement your reputation and jobs should line up smoothly. The challenge after that is to progress up the ladder through the ranks to wherever you are aspiring to be. At the start of your career, you don't really have the option of choosing your jobs depending on scripts, crew, location and position but as you gain more experience and status, you can choose projects you are passionate about or jobs that work well with your work-life balance.

Good luck with your endeavours and who knows, maybe one day I'll bump into you on set.

Jennifer Leacey
Director/Assistant Director

The Great Gatsby, Moulin Rouge, Wanted, Wonderland

What was your first job in the film industry?

Art Department Runner on a film clip for INXS that was being filmed at the now defunct Phoenician Club in Sydney. My first AD job was as a 3rd AD for PJ Voeten on a film called *Children of the Revolution*. I had never worn a radio before, had no real idea what an extra was, and as for cast trailers and winnebagos – it was all double dutch. I ended up learning tons and never wanting to give up.

Did you study?

Not as an Assistant Director – it was all on-the-job, seat-of-your pants training.

However, when I was confident and 100% sure of moving into directing, I went to film school to do directing as a postgrad course (and absolutely loved it).

What is one piece of advice you would give to someone starting in the film industry?

Ask yourself this one question... am I tolerant towards others? If yes, then pursue. If no, then you will be fighting an uphill battle within yourself and towards others every single day you go to work.

What was your favourite job or best memory?
A big memory for me is a conversation I shared with Donald Sutherland one day at work and his subsequent gratefulness about my openness, and admittance of how he used it to shape a performance. A lightbulb moment in a number of ways.

Why would someone pursue a career as a Director?
To share stories.

Did you always want to be a Director or did that develop as you furthered your AD career?
It definitely developed as I observed more and became more confident in understanding the craft. However, telling stories and sharing views has always been at my core.

GLOSSARY

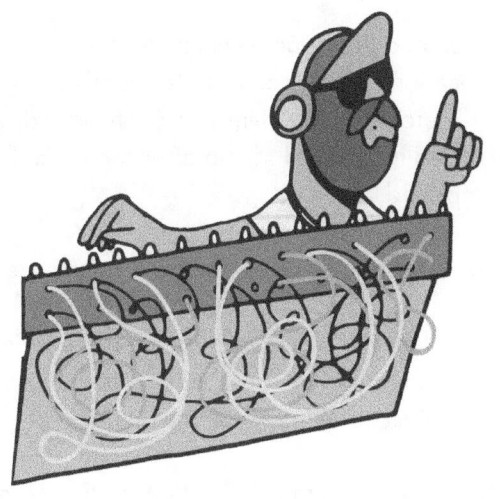

Abby Singer Shot – The second last camera setup of the day. Named after the renowned Assistant Director, Abby Singer, who always called the last two shots, giving the crew time to start packing up their gear knowing they were almost at wrap.

Australian Business Number (ABN) – An 11-digit number that identifies your business as a registered trading business to the government and other businesses. You need an ABN if you are a freelancer, invoicing clients for your work.

Above-the-line – Refers to the breakdown of a film budget where the costs associated with key creative elements are calculated. This section includes the fees for Director, Writer, Producer and key cast costs.

ADR (Automatic Dialogue Replacement) – Used when the original location sound recording is unusable, has errors or does not match how the film has been edited. The artist is re-recorded in a sound studio after the initial filming has been completed.

Anamorphic – Shooting widescreen format on a standard 35mm film frame. Nowadays, this usually refers to anamorphic lenses that squeeze a widescreen image into a standard 35mm frame. These lenses allow DOPs to shoot widescreen films on 35mm equipment.

Apple Box – An extremely versatile set of nestled timber boxes carried by the grips for raising equipment, sitting on and anything else you can think of.

A/T (Afternoon Tea) – A meal break scheduled five hours after the conclusion of lunch. Often A/T is taken on wrap to not disrupt the shooting momentum.

Atmos – Anything added to the air to create a different atmosphere look. Usually smoke or haze created by the SFX department.

Atmos Track – A recording of all the white noise in a location without any dialogue or sound effects.

Back On – Break's over! Get back to work.

Bazooka – A camera mount similar to a tripod but only has one centre shaft that raises the camera up and down.

Beat – A measure of time, usually a second.

Below-the-line – All the technical elements of a budget that isn't included in the above-the-line costs. This includes crew, locations, equipment rental, travel and art department costs.

Blocking – Early stages of rehearsing a scene. The Director works with the cast to place everybody in the set and walk through movements and actions.

Box Schedule – A schedule summarised into a box calendar layout. Great for crew to have a quick look at locations and dates for the shoot.

Box Rental – A personal item rented by the production company for a set weekly price. E.g. A laptop or standby kit.

Bump Up – An extra obtains a pay rise for the day when they receive direction from the Director as opposed to the ADs. This may include receiving some lines of dialogue or specific actions.

Buttoned On – Somebody is accidentally pressing the button on his or her radio microphone. Can be from sitting on it or carrying something that's pressing against the button. Sometimes this also happens when the radio headset gets dusty or wet and jams on. It results in your radio jamming the channel signal and everyone on channel hearing what you are saying.

Call Sheet (Callie) – The call sheet has everything you need to know about each day. Read this over and over before asking any obvious questions. Most likely the answer is in there somewhere. Call sheets for the next day are issued as hard copies by the ADs on wrap and also emailed by the production office in case you don't receive one on set.

Call time (Call) – The time of day an individual is scheduled to begin work.

Camera Left/Camera Right – The direction of left and right in relation to the direction the camera is facing. Usually opposite the subject's left and right.

Check The Gate – Called out after a take that the Director is satisfied with, for the 1st AC to check the internal part of the film camera called the gate. They check for any signs that may cause the film to be unusable in that previous take. Nowadays, as we use digital media rather than film stock, some people use the term 'check the chip' as there is no film gate but a camera hard drive. The 1st AC may playback the last take on the camera to ensure there were no technical faults.

Cine Saddle – A bag shaped like a saddle used to rest the camera on when shooting on the ground or when the camera is on the operator's lap.

Closed Set – Only the bare necessity of crew are permitted around camera for a closed set as the scene involves sensitive content. Usually nudity, sex scenes or highly emotional scenes.

Continuous Day (French Hours) – A ten-hour shooting day is worked without stopping for a sit down meal break. A boxed meal is provided on the run for crew members by craft services. This allows the production to utilise as much viable shooting time in the day without slowing down for a break.

Count to 10 – Pause or wait for a small amount of time until a decision is made.

Coverage – The list of different shots to complete the scene. E.g. The coverage of this scene involves a wide establishing shot, a close-up and a reverse.

Cowboys – A shot that is framed just above the knees of the subject.

Craft Services (Crafties) – A food truck that supplies snacks and food to the crew between meal breaks. They also serve the boxed meals on continuous days.

Crew Call – The time of day shooting is scheduled to begin for the day.

Crossing – Called out as you walk in front of the lens if the camera operator is lining up the shot. Courteous to let them know you will block their shot momentarily but are passing through.

Cutaway – A shot of something that isn't directly related to the action sequence. E.g. A cutaway shot of a clock, as a student rushes down a hallway late to class. Often cutaway shots will be left to the end of filming in the day or schedule as they don't require all the key personnel to film them.

Day For Night (D4N) – Shooting during daylight hours when the story is set at night-time. Usually filming occurs inside where the windows can be blacked out to create the illusion of night outside.

Day Player – An actor who is only scheduled for a day or two of filming because they only appear briefly in a small amount of scenes.

Deal Memo – A summary of your negotiations of your contract. This includes your weekly rate, overtime conditions, and any additional allowances like car or phone payments. This is signed by yourself and a production representative and forms the basis of your contract.

DFI (Don't Follow Instruction) – Stand down, don't do what I just told you to do, something has changed so it's not needed anymore, standby for new instructions.

Dingle – A piece of cut-off foliage to provide the lighting effect of a tree shadow on the subject.

Dirty – Something is in the foreground of the shot. E.g. An actor's shoulder or some set dressing.

DMB (Delayed Meal Break) – A delayed meal break occurs when the crew breaks for lunch more than six hours after the end of their last meal break, or whatever is stated in your contract. This mainly occurs at lunch when the Director or 1st AD thinks it's important to continue to get this shot before breaking. A DMB incurs a monetary penalty as stated in your contract. Be sure to write this on your timesheet so accounts know to pay you for this, but the ADs are the official timekeepers of when lunch is called, so accounts will go off their time.

Dolly – A specialised piece of equipment that the camera is mounted onto that slides along the dolly tracks. This is extremely heavy; avoid being too close to the grips when they are looking for a hand carrying this up the stairs.

Double – A person that looks similar and has a comparable build to an actor to be used on camera when the actor is not available. Commonly used for close-ups of hands, over shoulder and back of head shots. It can also be a trained stunt double who is used when the action is too dangerous for the actor to perform.

Dutch Tilt – Tilting the frame so the horizontal axis is not level with the horizon.

Essentials – Special car parking for equipment trucks and vehicles that are required to be as close to the filming location as possible. The spaces are generally limited so this is not where you park your car.

Electronic Press Kit (EPK) – Similar to behind the scenes footage, the EPK consists of interviews with key cast and HODs and is used in promoting the project.

Eyeline – Where an actor looks relative to camera. This may be adjusted on different camera setups to ensure the shots can be cut together smoothly.

Final Checks (Checks and Shoot) – Called by the ADs just before cameras roll for makeup and costume to do a final look at the cast to ensure everything is as it should be for filming.

First Position (Ones) – The place where an actor starts in the scene. They may then have a move to a second position and so on.

Flag On the Play – After calling 'moving on' but then realising we need to do the take again for various reasons. Crew may call 'flag on the play' so people pause and discuss the issue before doing another take or moving on.

Flash – Called out when a camera flash is used when taking photos. Identifies that the flash of light was from a camera and not an unexpected occurrence in one of the lights such as a globe blowing.

Foley – Foley sounds are added in post-production to add sound effects to any action that wasn't recorded in the shoot. E.g. Footsteps or a door closing.

GoBo (Go Between) – A cutout lighting effect created between the lighting source and subject. Usually a rotating disk with holes cut out creating an interesting lighting effect.

Going Again – Said after a take meaning they will shoot that take again. Everything will reset to where it started and cameras will roll again.

Green – An inexperienced or new crew member. E.g. 'That crew member is a bit green.'

High Hat/Low Hat – A low camera mount that sits just off the ground.

Head of Department (HOD) – The person in charge of their department. Represents their department at production meetings and location recces. Sometimes referred to as 'the grown ups'.

Hollywood Wrap – When you are in the same location for multiple days of filming so you are able to leave equipment where it is on wrap rather than packing into the truck.

Hot Brick – A fully charged radio battery.

Hot Set – A set that is currently in use for filming or needs to be left as is because filming will return there in the near future. Don't touch or move the props or set dressing.

House Power – Using the location's power as opposed to power supplied by the electrics generator. Always good to check with the electrics department that it's ok to plug into house power.

Indie (Independent Film) – a film that is not produced by one of the major studios.

In the Can – Describes having captured the take or scene. The term is coined from shooting film stock that, when exposed, was placed in a film can.

Lock it Down/Make Safe – Often called by the ADs to let crew know they need the set to be quiet for rehearsing or filming that's about to take place. An AD may call, 'Lock it down' with a crew member replying, 'Making safe' to let them know there will be a bit of noise before they can be silent while they make safe on the equipment they are using.

LUT (Look Up Table) – An approximate colour grade that can be incorporated into the camera workflow or video playback to show roughly what the finished colour graded image will look like.

Magic Hour or Golden Hour – Approximately an hour's worth of light after sunrise and also before sunset where the height of the sun in the sky produces a beautiful soft light that is more red in colour than when the sun is higher in the sky. DOPs use this beautiful natural light creatively in exteriors to create a different look and feel to the scene where they deem appropriate.

Market Rates - The median rate a position is paid for a standard working week if the conditions of overtime, turnarounds and penalties are similar. These rates should be a base for your negotiations for each job but if you are inexperienced, expect your rate to be lower until you get a few jobs under your belt. The various unions often publish market rates on their websites so you can do a bit of research before your negotiations begin.

Martini Shot – The last camera setup of the day. Announced on set so everyone knows to pack up any equipment not in use. Called this as the next 'shot' is from a glass.

Master – A camera setup that runs the entire scene and keeps all characters in view. Often used as an establishing shot of the scene. Most directors will begin by shooting the master coverage of a scene and then move onto the closer coverage of singles, etc.

Method Acting – An acting technique that involves the actor staying in character even when the cameras aren't rolling.

Mexican Reverse – When one shot is done looking in a certain direction and then the reverse of that shot is cheated still looking in that same direction, called the Mexican reverse. The background can be manipulated slightly by a different camera angle or moving the set dressing. A DOP will choose to shoot this way due to the lighting available or unusable backgrounds at the location. The term originates from Westerns that were shot on Mexican beaches where they could only look into the sand dunes as the opposite direction was the ocean.

MOS (Mute On Sound or Mit Out Sound) – Rolling cameras without recording sound. MOS is written on the slate so those in post-production know there are no sound files to sync with the takes.

MOW (Make Own Way) – An actor or crew member will transport themselves to set for their call time.

Mud Map – A detailed map of truck parking, equipment storage and essential items of a shooting location.

New Deal – Moving on to a new camera setup for that scene.

NG (No Good) – Often used by crew to signal the last take was not usable for some reason. E.g. The sound was NG.

Off Screen – The actor is not in the camera frame but is still required to be on set for an eyeline or to deliver their dialogue for the other actors.

One Liner – A summarised version of the full shooting schedule with each scene reduced to one line.

Open Radio – A radio without a headset attached. Everyone in close proximity to that radio can hear the dialogue on that channel.

Over Shoulder – A shot framed looking over the subject's shoulder. Often used in interviews or intimate conversations.

Pancake – A set of nestled timber boxes that are thinner than apple boxes but used for similar purposes.

PAYG (Pay As You Go Tax) – A taxation system that allows your tax to be paid periodically through your employer. Each pay check will have a portion of tax taken out and paid so you don't receive a large tax bill at the end of the financial year.

Petty Cash (PC)/Float – A sum of money loaned to certain crew members to cover everyday purchases for production. It's extremely important to keep all receipts and submit your forms neatly to accounts. All money is returned and balanced with receipts when the float is closed with production.

Per Diem – A daily allowance for costs incurred while filming on location. Usually for food and laundry.

Picking Up – Doing the take again but starting midway through the scene from a specified spot indicated by the Director or Script Supervisor.

Picture Wrap – The completion of filming with an actor or item for the entire shooting schedule.

Plate Shots – Used in visual effects to fill in backgrounds or to composite shots together. These could be cityscapes, travelling shots for sim-trav replacement or empty frames of the scene when a visual effect composite is necessary.

POV (Point of View) – A shot taken from the view of the subject. Normally what the actor is looking at but can be the POV of any item. E.g. An animal's POV looking up at its owner.

Pre-Call – When a department or individual has a call time earlier than the crew call.

Pre-Frame – The Camera Operator may set a frame for the actor to walk into. The operator may ask the actor to stand on their mark just before cameras roll to ensure their framing is in the correct position. The actor then starts out of frame and enters the pre-frame.

Pulled Call – Call times have been brought earlier by a specific amount of time. E.g. 'All calls pulled by 30 minutes' means your call time is now 30 minutes earlier than what is printed on the call sheet.

Pushed Call – Call times have been delayed by a specific amount of time. E.g. 'All calls pushed by 30 minutes' means your call time is now 30 minutes later than what was printed on the call sheet.

Residuals – Additional compensation paid to certain creators, technicians and onscreen performers for use of the project beyond what they were originally contracted for. E.g. A performer may be paid for the theatrical release of a film, but then receives residuals when the film is released to DVD and aired on TV. These come in the form of cheques in the mail and everyone loves them if you are lucky enough to receive them!

Runner – Runners are managed by the office to pick up and deliver almost anything you can think of. They are not here to pick up your dry cleaning (unless you are the Producer) but they can be great in organising any pickups and deliveries between the office and set. Get friendly with the runners and they'll be able to help you out in so many ways. Rushes/Dailies – The footage shot from the day. Often distributed to the Producer, Director and DOP for viewing throughout the shoot.

Recce – Visiting a location before shooting commences there to plan and work through any issues that may arise from the location. Multiple location recces will take place in pre-production with most HODs present to ensure no time is wasted during the shoot.

Sherhearsal – Used to describe shooting when a rehearsal is needed but they would like to roll cameras.

Side of the Line – The camera placement in reference to the 180-degree rule. E.g. A Director may ask a DOP, 'What side of the line do you want to be on?' when discussing coverage of a scene.

Sides – Pocket sized script printouts of the scenes that are scheduled for the day of shooting distributed to those that require them on set.

SimTrav (Simulated Travel) – A technique used to shoot what appears to be travelling vehicle shots without the vehicle actually moving. Green screens are used with the travelling background added later from plate shots. Multiple lights are set up to create the illusion that the characters are in a travelling vehicle.

Singles – A close up shot containing just one character.

Slabbed – You now owe the crew a case of beer. This can be a result of your phone going off while rolling or some action that directly inconvenienced another crew member. E.g. You parked in the wrong spot in the morning blocking access for the essential trucks to park.

Slate (Clapper Board) – The clapper board used by the 2nd ACs to put an ID on each take so the editor can easily see what scene this shot is for and what take it is. It is also used to sync the sound between the camera takes and sound rushes during post-production.

Speed – Termed from when cameras and sound recorders were film based, means the machine has reached the desired frames per second. Is usually called by the Sound Recordist after turnover to signal they are recording sound.

Spraying – When spraying any aerosol such as hairspray or water around the camera, it's considerate to call 'spraying' so the camera department can either cover up the lens or turn the camera away from where you are so nothing goes on the lens.

Squib – A small explosive device used by SFX to simulate gunshots and small explosions. Can be used on someone's body or an object.

Stand-in (2nd Team) – A person of the same height, shape and skin tone of an actor used in place of the actor while the shot is lit and camera moves are rehearsed. The stand-in will read the script and know the lines just as the actor does so they can run the scene for any camera moves or timings if needed.

Stinger – A single extension power cord left 'hot' by the electrics for occasional use.

Stunt Loading – An additional payment given to a stunt performer for performing a dangerous stunt. The amount will be decided by the Stunt Coordinator and added to the daily production report.

Sushi – A small rectangle piece of wood used by the grips to raise, support or level items.

Swing Gang – A separate group of crew that come to relocate vehicles and equipment trucks or redress a set when the shooting crew have wrapped.

Switch (Switch to 2, Switch to Chat) – Change radio channels to the designated chat channel. Usually used by the ADs to avoid too much chat happening on the ever-busy channel 1 on radios.

Tail Slate/End Slate – The clapper board is added at the end of a take rather than at the beginning. The slate is turned upside down or 90 degrees to identify it is a tail slate.

Texas Switch – The swapping of an element off camera during the middle of a take. Commonly used for switching a live animal to a stuffed animal or stunt double to a cast member during the take. Allows the full scene to be played out even when dangerous circumstances prevent it.

The Lot – The film studio. 'Are you on the lot?'

Track – Looks like railway track and is laid for the camera dolly to move along. Be careful not to bump into or trip on this when it's laid as the grips will be most unhappy and have to relay it.

Two Shot – A medium shot containing two characters.

Unit Base – This is where the makeup, costume and cast trailers are located. Usually crew parking is here as well and meals are generally served at unit base. It's the largest base and first point of call when arriving for work.

What's your 20? – 'Where are you, what's your location?'

When are we back on? – 'When is the end of lunch, how long until we are needed back at work?'

Wild Lines – The lines of dialogue from the scene recorded separately after a scene is complete where the Sound Recordist wasn't happy with the sound atmosphere. E.g. Loud fans were being used by SFX that prevented a clean audio track to be recorded.

Wrap – End something, usually the end of the day of filming but can be used as wrap on a scene, actor or item.

Wrap Party – A party for cast and crew of the film at the completion of shooting.

10/100 or 10/1 – going to the bathroom.

10/200 or 10/2 – think about it…

$5 Friday – A $5 raffle amongst the crew where the winner takes the lot. Each ticket goes directly into the pool. Usually drawn on wrap by a guest or the Director. Sometimes this is modified to $10 Saturday or various other versions on special occasions.

86 – to remove or get rid of an item. E.g. 86 the left vase.

APPENDIX

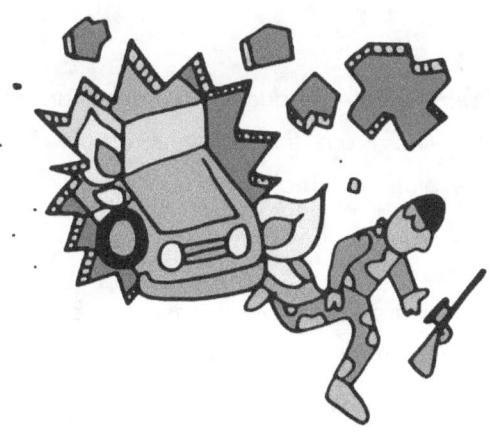

I haven't read every book out there on filmmaking but here are a few of my favourites that will definitely help you develop your career. I personally buy about two of these types of books every six months to keep a good reading pile stocked and continue to complement everything I learn on set with these great insights and guides.

Scriptwriting
Save The Cat!: The Last Book on Screenwriting You'll Ever Need – Blake Snyder

Directing
Making Movies - Sidney Lumet
Hitchcock - Francois Truffaut (Interviews)
The Name Above The Title - Frank Capra

Producing
So You Want To Be A Producer – Lawrence Turman
Hope for Film: From the Frontline of the Independent Cinema Revolutions – Ted Hope

Crew
Hollywood Game Plan: How to Land a Job in Film, TV, or Digital Entertainment – Carole Kirschner

Business
How To Win Friends and Influence People – Dale Carnegie
Never Eat Alone: And Other Secrets to Success, One Relationship at a Time – Keith Ferazzi

Film Festivals

Chris Gore's Ultimate Film Festival Survival Guide: The Essential Companion for Filmmakers and Festival-Goers – Chris Gore

Bios

Rebel without a Crew: Or How a 23-Year-Old Filmmaker With $7,000 Became a Hollywood Player - Robert Rodriguez
Walt Disney – Bob Thomas

Coffee Table

The Wes Anderson Collection – Wes Anderson, Matt Zoller Seitz, Eric Anderson
Saturday Night Live. The Book – Alison Castle

ACKNOWLEDGEMENTS

This book was a collective effort, as all books are, and I am so grateful for those that surrounded me during this journey.

JENNY WEBB

My gorgeous wife! You've encouraged me to finish this off and turned my occasionally boring text into something much more palatable. I love you. Thanks for being so involved in getting this project completed.

MUM

Mum's been critiquing my grammar since primary school, so when I finished my draft, of course she got the job of correcting every comma and apostrophe. She's also a pretty good Mum.

ALLAN WRATH

Allan, nobody can illustrate quite like you. Thanks so much for designing the awesome cover. Everyone agrees – they only bought this book because of the cover.

TESS GUINERY & ANDY INGLIS

Thanks for bouncing design ideas back and forth and turning my dodgy templates into typography masterpieces.

ANDREW PANTE, CHRIS TURNER & JACQUI KING

Thanks to Andrew and Chris. They were lumped with me for work experience and were kind enough to teach me everything I didn't know.

Jacqui King took a risk and hired me for my very first AD job and I haven't looked back since. Thanks Jacqui.

CONTRIBUTORS

Thanks to George Miller, Mark Huffam, Lesley Vanderwalt, Simon Duggan, PJ Voeten, Dan Oliver, Kyle Gardiner, Ben Osmo, Jennifer Leacey and Janty Yates.

Your contribution and insight into the industry are invaluable. Thank you for not only teaching me your craft along the way but for being so honest and open in these interviews.

JESUS

I am constantly grateful that you've enabled me to work in this crazy industry and pursue the dreams you have given me. Thank you.

POZIBLE SUPPORTERS

A massive thanks to all the wonderful people who supported *Setlife* from the start.

Cathy Amies • Cameron Ambridge • Charnstar Anderson Taylor Bates • Jesse Blayney • Chrissy Burow • Shaun Cantwell • Xander Collier • Jay Corry • Ben Dickinson Luke Dunham • Simon Edds • Claire Elissa • Eamon Farren James Fraser • Patrick Frischknecht • Harri Gilbert • Shayla Girdler • Natalie Greaves • Caleb Guinery • Ally Henville Isabel Hilton • Ben Hughes • David Innes • Ciaron Jackson Bryan Jordan • Kris Keevers • Brad Kendrick • Amy Kings Dan Mackenzie • Alistair MacKenzie • Killian Maguire • Viv McDonald • Paul Micallef • Daniel Millar • Nicholas Molteno Nick Mutton • Mike O'Connor • Jasmine Pascoe • Paul Pederson • Jessica Pryke • Rachael Greenup • Briana Rayner Michael Reidy • Matthew Samperi • Joshua Searle • Andrew Sears Andrew Seaton • Naomi Sharp • Harri Sharp • Brendan Shaw • Bekki Shearer • David Shirley • Adam Signorelli Morgan Smallbone • Katrina Thomlinson • Daniel Thone Christopher Turner • Joe Vasey • Ben Webb • Felicity Wheen

ABOUT THE AUTHOR

At work...

Matt Webb has racked up an impressive slate of projects during his time in the film industry. Having landed his first role as 3rd Assistant Director on the Australian TV drama *Rescue Special Ops*, Matt has never looked back. Working as an Assistant Director on films including *The Great Gatsby*, *Mad Max: Fury Road*, *Pirates of the Caribbean* and *Alien: Covenant*, has cemented Matt's outstanding reputation in the film industry. Adding to the list of feature films under his belt are a variety of TV shows, TVCs, short films and music videos.

At home...

Matt lives in Sydney's Northern Beaches with his wife Jenny. When he isn't on set, he loves surfing and snowboarding.

Film/TV Credits:

Alien: Covenant

Mad Max: Fury Road

The Great Gatsby

Hacksaw Ridge

Backtrack

Banished

Felony

Down Under

Goddess

Modern Family

Pirates of the Carribean 5

Thor: Ragnarok

Truth

Not Suitable For Children

Puberty Blues

Love Is Now

Rescue Special Ops